SOCIAL MEDIA MARKETING

A COMPREHENSIVE GUIDE TO SETTING UP AN EFFECTIVE SOCIAL MEDIA MARKETING STRATEGY

WILLIAM ROBERT SMITH

CONTENTS

PROLOGUE

"Social media is here. It's not going away; not a passing fad. Be where your customers are: in social media."

LORI RUFF, SPEAKER AND AUTHOR.

Many companies, small and big, look at successful social media campaigns and wish they were theirs. The biggest mistake they make is trying to be like the successful brands they've seen on social media platforms without taking their time to understand how they got there. You are probably a victim too.

You rushed into creating a business account on different social media platforms and started marketing your products. However, four months down the line, you were not making any progress. Well, have you ever heard that *if you fail to plan, you are planning to fail*? That's what is happening.

It might comfort you to know that you are not alone! Many people have been in the same predicament and came out of it successfully. You need to take a few steps back and ask yourself if you really know what you are doing. I know you have discovered you probably don't know enough.

This is where this comprehensive piece on social media marketing comes in. The information shared here is unique because it is a collection of years of experience that includes learning from many mistakes. You are lucky and wiser because you will not be learning from your mistakes. After reading this book, I can guarantee that you will see some changes in your marketing efforts.

First, the book will introduce you to the concept of social media marketing. This is critical because it will give you a different perspective of the social media platforms you use daily for personal delight. After that, it lets you in on the *Fundamentals of Social Media Marketing*. Here, you will discover there are five pillars your social media marketing should stand upon. Chapter 3 will then reveal the benefits social media marketing will bring to your business to whet your appetite.

With that information in mind, you will be ready to dig deeper. Chapter 4 takes you through the top-rated *Social Media Marketing Platforms*. This chapter will help you understand how the different social media platforms work and the demography of users. You will discover that there is some science behind the trending content you see on social media platforms like Facebook, Instagram, and TikTok. After that, Chapter 5 reminds you that *Email Marketing* is still an important strategy. You will learn the different types of email marketing, tools, and how the strategy works. You will then understand the importance of having a website for your brand in Chapter 6 and how to incorporate it into your social media marketing strategy.

Chapter 7 will help you understand the concept of *Social Media Marketing Strategy*. The information here will help you to start piecing together the information you have learned in the previous chapters. After that, Chapter 8 introduces the importance of Search Engine Optimization in Social Media marketing. Reading this chapter will give you an understanding of how you can effectively combine SEO and social media.

How will you know if your strategy is working? Chapter 9 discusses how you can take advantage of *Social Media Analytics* to measure your progress and refine your strategy. You will discover that your Social Media Marketing Strategy is a living document that you should continually update based on new data. After collecting all that information, Chapter 10 will encourage you to get to work by offering practical steps you should follow to create your first Social Media Marketing Strategy. Chapter 11 is the icing on your social media marketing strategy cake. You will discover the fundamentals of

Affiliate Marketing and how to tap into its potential. Furthermore, you will discover the current trends in affiliate marketing.

Reading this book will help you take slow but steady steps in your social media marketing efforts. The mantra is to start small, learn, and grow. Ready? Let's dig in!

CHAPTER 1
SOCIAL MEDIA MARKETING - GETTING STARTED

Social media is a famous term that many people commonly use. Some users do not really understand what they are talking about when they use the term. Understand what social media means before delving deeper into social media marketing.

WHAT IS SOCIAL MEDIA?

Social media refers to a computer technology that allows people to share ideas and information via virtual networks (Hudson, 2020). It is Internet-based and offers swift electronic communication of content, including documents, photos, videos, and personal information. Users can engage with social media using their computer, tablet, or smartphone through web-based software or applications. In other words, social media is a digital tool that enables its users to create and share content with the public quickly.

Initially, social media was meant to be a way for people to interact with family and friends. However, businesses later adopted it to harness its power to help reach out to current and potential clients. Social media's power is its capability to connect and share information with people globally. You can also reach many people simultaneously.

Data from Investopedia shows there are over 3.8 billion social media users worldwide (Dollarhide, 2021). It is also a highly dynamic field where new apps are launched almost yearly. Experts also predict that the number of social media users in the U.S. could reach 257 million by 2023.

HOW DOES SOCIAL MEDIA WORK?

The function of different social media tools varies as there are different types of websites and applications. For most of them, you can start by creating a user profile by providing a name and a valid email address. After that, you can create and share different forms of content.

You can also look for other social media users whose content you may want to follow or share your thoughts on. Depending on the social media tool you are using, you can interact with other users by following them, adding them as a friend, or subscribing to other users' pages.

Social media platforms also use "feeds" to enable users to scroll through content. In this sense, social media companies use algorithms to determine the content that appears on your feeds and the order in which it appears based on the data on your profile. Your feed will also include content from users you follow and entities running paid promotions.

SIX MAIN TYPES OF SOCIAL MEDIA

There are multiple types of social media, and many services can fit into different categories. Here are the main types of social media with their examples.

Social Networks

Social networks provide a platform for people to connect and share ideas and content with other users having similar tastes and interests. Examples of social networks include Twitter and Facebook. You can also consider LinkedIn as a social network despite appearing to be more professional.

Media Sharing Networks

Media networks allow their users to distribute content such as videos and photographs. Popular examples under this category include YouTube,

Snapchat, TikTok, and Instagram. YouTube allows users to upload a video they have created, and other users can comment, dislike, or like the video. Additionally, if a user loves your content, they can subscribe to your channel so that when you upload new content, it will appear in their feed.

Discussion Forums

Discussion forums are the perfect outlet for posts that can ignite thorough discussions among users. You can leave detailed comments here. Other users can respond directly to your comments which allows organic growth of the conversation. The leading discussion forums are Quora and Reddit.

Bookmarking & Content Curation Networks

Bookmarking and content curation networks enable users to discover, share, discuss and save different types of content and media. They are an essential tool to channelize brand awareness for businesses. It is an excellent tool for running social media marketing campaigns to generate website traffic and client engagement. Examples of these tools include Flipboard and Pinterest.

Consumer Review Networks

Consumer review networks are used to share, review and discover different information about different brands, services, and products. Suppose a business gets positive reviews on these networks; it makes their claims more credible because reviews on these networks serve as Social Proof.

Brands also use the issues raised by clients on these forums for more positive and productive outcomes for their business. These platforms allow users to review different products and services that they have used. Reviewing content adds value to brands because it influences more people to buy products or services. Popular examples include TripAdvisor, Zomato, and Yelp.

Blogging & Publishing Networks

Blogging and publishing networks are ideal for publishing, discovering, and commenting on posts, social media blogs, and other forms of web content. Content marketing is a popular way of targeting, attracting, engaging, and converting a target audience. Many use it as the basis for successful online marketing campaigns that play a significant role in Digital Marketing Campaigns' conversion funnels.

The traditional blogging platforms are Blogger and WordPress. There are also microblogging platforms such as Tumblr and Medium.

Social Media and Business

Social media platforms have emerged as critical parts of marketing for different businesses. However, for it to be successful, businesses must treat it with the care, respect, and attention they offer to other marketing efforts instead of treating it as an additional appendage.

WHAT IS SOCIAL MEDIA MARKETING?

Social Media Marketing (SMM) is using social media tools to build a company's brand, boost sales and drive traffic to their websites. Social media platforms enable companies to engage with current customers and reach new ones. Additionally, social media marketing uses purpose-built analytics that enables marketers to track the success of their efforts and identify more ways of engaging their users.

Social media marketing is a potent tool that has attracted the interest of businesses globally. Its main power comes from its unmatched capacity in three key areas of marketing: customer data, interaction, and connection (Hayes, 2022).

Customer Data

Running a properly-designed social media marketing campaign allows businesses to collect customer data. This is an invaluable resource if you are looking to boost your marketing outcomes. You do not have to be overwhelmed by the 3Vs of big data (velocity, variety, and volume). This is because SMM tools can extract customer data and turn it into actionable market analysis. Additionally, they can use the data for crowdsourcing new strategies.

Interaction

Social media offers businesses a dynamic way to interact with their users. For example, there is direct and passive communication such as "liking." This allows businesses to take advantage of free advertising opportunities from electronic word-of-mouth (eWOM). In addition, eWOM is a critical driver of consumer decisions, and since the interactions happen on the social network, they are measurable. For example, a business can measure its *"social equity"* (a term for the return on investment) from social media marketing campaigns.

Connection

First, social media enables businesses to connect with customers in ways that were previously deemed impossible. It also offers businesses an astonishing range of avenues to connect with their target audiences. For instance, they can use content platforms like YouTube, microblogging services like Twitter, and social sites like Facebook.

HOW SOCIAL MEDIA MARKETING WORKS

Several critical factors govern how social media marketing works. You must consider these factors as you create your social media marketing strategy.

Social Media Marketing Action Plan

For your SMM strategy to be effective, it has to be more targeted. In this sense, you need a proper action plan that contains an execution framework and performance metrics. Here are some creative tips for developing an effective SMM action plan:

- Align your SMM goals to unambiguous business objectives
- Research your target audience (age, location, industry, job title, income, and interests)
- Analyze your competition (look at their failures and successes)
- Audit your current SMM's failures and successes
- Create a calendar for your SMM content delivery
- Produce best-in-class content
- Evaluate performance and fine-tune your SMM strategy accordingly

Customer Relationship Management

Social media marketing offers two kinds of interactions: customer-to-customer and business-to-customer. These forms of interaction offer advantages that allow targeted customer relationship management tools. Whereas traditional marketing usually tracks customer value mainly by capturing purchase activity, SMM has the capacity to track customer value directly (from purchases) and indirectly (from product referrals).

Shareable Content

Businesses can also convert SMM's augmented interconnectedness into "sticky" content creation. Sticky content is the marketing term for eye-catching content that engages clients at first glimpse. The content encourages them to buy products and also makes them want to share the content.

This kind of eWOM advertising allows business advertisements to reach audiences that would have been inaccessible. In addition, it provides the inherent endorsement of someone the recipient knows and probably trusts. Consequently, creating shareable content is critical for social media marketing to drive growth.

Earned Media

Social media marketing also offers businesses an efficient way to reap the benefits of a different kind of earned media. This is the term used to refer to brand exposure that comes from a method other than paid advertising. The earned media comes from product reviews and recommendations by current users.

Viral Marketing

Viral marketing is another SMM strategy that depends on the audience to create the message. This sales technique tries to trigger the rapid spread of eWOM product information. The marketing message is considered viral once it spreads beyond the intended target audience to the general public.

Customer Segmentation

Customer segmentation is much more refined in SMM than on the usual marketing channels. Therefore, companies can focus their marketing resources on precise target audiences.

Tracking Metrics

The most critical SMM metrics should focus on:

- **Engagement:** such as clicks, comments, shares, and likes
- **Impressions:** measures how many times an SMM post shows up
- **Reach/virality:** meaning the number of unique views an SMM post has attracted
- **Share of voice:** measures how far your brand reaches
- **Referrals:** how do users land on your site?
- **Conversions:** when users make purchases on a site
- **Response rate/time:** how often and how fast the brand responds to client messages

As a rule of thumb, align each business goal to a relevant metric to help determine the metrics to track in the sea of data generated by social media. For example, if your business goal is to use the SMM campaign to grow conversions by 15% in three months, use a social media analytics tool that measures your campaign's effectiveness against a specific target. These metrics will be covered in detail later in this book.

TIPS FOR SOCIAL MEDIA MARKETING

At this point, you probably feel like you are ready to get started with SMM! Here are some tips that will come in handy.

Your content should be diverse

By now, you know that content reigns supreme in matters of social media marketing. Ensure you post regularly, and your content is precious that your target audience will find interesting and helpful.

Some content tips you can consider are:

- News on local industries
- Quick tips and how-tos
- Contests, polls, and questions
- Data and insights
- Announcements and updates

Additionally, you should use the variety of formats social media offers, such as livestreams, stories, images, videos, and stores.

Consistency is key

Using social media for marketing allows businesses to protect their brands on different social media platforms. Each platform has its own unique voice and environment, but your brand's core identity should remain consistent.

After posting, participate

Remember that social media platforms are communities. Focus on who shares your content, and interact with them. Respond to comments, comment on user posts, like, share, post polls, run livestreams, and repost others' content.

Consider using content creation tools

Contrary to popular belief, Instagram is not the most visual social media platform; they all are! Therefore, for your brand to be visible in a person's feed, your posts must include photos, attractive visuals, illustrations, and text turned into art. Luckily, multiple content creation tools offer templates and features that enable you to create professional visuals effortlessly.

Repurpose, repost, and recycle

Since the social media space is jam-packed, brands must post great content regularly. Use the three Rs as your guiding principle to achieve this:

- **Repurpose:** Create your social media posts from a customer review, split a blog post into a thread of Tweets, and break down a case study into the customer limelight on Instagram. Other repurposing ideas include turning a webinar deck into a carousel post on LinkedIn, among other creative ideas.
- **Report:** You should do this in moderation. Nonetheless, this is an excellent way of filling gaps in your content calendar. For example, you can repost on Instagram or retweet user-generated and influencer content. You can also curate content from respected sources and share the links in your social media posts.
- **Recycle:** You can post your TikTok videos and Instagram Reels on YouTube or re-share your best-performing blog posts monthly to

reach new followers. Alternatively, you can add your Facebook Live recordings to your brand's YouTube channel.

Curate your brand's feed

Every brand works day and night in ways they can feature in other people's feeds. Nevertheless, they usually forget that they can derive value from their own. Keep tabs on your competitors by following them and gathering ideas on how you can adapt your current strategy. Identify any gaps in your strategy.

Additionally, follow influencers to be acquainted with the latest trends and increase your knowledge. You can also follow brands with whom you share values or that have excellent content strategies to get outside-the-box ideas and inspiration.

Use analytics to measure success

You must track data to determine the success of your social media marketing strategies. Google Analytics is an excellent tool you can consider to measure your SMM techniques. It will also help you determine which strategies to drop. Use hashtags on your SMM campaign to allow you to monitor them properly. Also, ensure you are using analytics within all the social platforms you are using. This approach gives you more insight into which social content is performing exceptionally well with your target audience.

Take advantage of paid social media advertising

Social media advertising is very cost-effective. If you plan correctly, you can reach your target audience at a very economical cost. Furthermore, most social media platforms provide granular targeting abilities that allow you to focus your budget on the people interested in your brand.

Current Social Media Trends Marketers should consider

As mentioned earlier, the social media space is highly dynamic. As a result, brands are continually revising their strategies for promoting products and services. These trends result from examining many top brands to learn the business-to-business and business-to-consumer trends.

Here are the top six research-backed social media trends marketers can take advantage of ("The 2022 Social Media Trends Report," 2022):

- **TikTok has become dominant in the social media space:** According to reports, TikTok has registered unprecedented growth. It is easy to assume that its popularity is a passing cloud. However, experts believe the platform offers unique opportunities for brands to engage with consumers directly. Top brands such as the NBA are already using the app to reach new audiences.
- **Businesses use social media to reach new audiences:** most businesses use social media to reach new audiences. They use these platforms to boost brand awareness/reach new audiences.
- **Companies have made more dedicated social media hires.** Social media can be a critical tool for generating revenue. For example, reports suggest that over 75% of people claim that user-generated content significantly impacted their purchasing decisions (Needle, 2022). In this regard, more companies are making more dedicated social media hires.
- **Augmented reality has emerged as the most preferred way for consumers to try products:** it is becoming progressively more common for brands to use AR to allow customers to test their products before purchasing.
- **Brands operating in the B2B space have put more investment into Instagram and Twitter:** While the two platforms are not new, marketers see an increase in ROI across both. Their success has attracted more marketers to invest in the platforms.
- **Influencer marketing is becoming of age:** influencer marketing has grown in the past two years. As you closely watch the social media space, you will discover an increased use of influencers by different brands. This approach is prevalent in TikTok, where brands might find it challenging to establish themselves.

KEY TAKEAWAYS

- Social media is undoubtedly a massive marketing tool brands cannot ignore.

- Brands that take a professional approach to social media marketing will get the desired results.
- You need to understand the core pillars of social media and the fundamentals of social media marketing to run a successful social media marketing campaign.
- Brands can no longer treat social media marketing as extra work for the marketing department. It needs to be given the same weight as other departments.

Now that you have a rough idea of what social media marketing is, it is time to take the conversation to a deeper level and look at **Chapter 2: Fundamentals of Social Media Marketing**.

CHAPTER 2
FUNDAMENTALS OF SOCIAL MEDIA MARKETING

When marketers are designing marketing programs, a key area they consider is how they will deliver their messages. Social media has made their work more manageable since it allows them to spread the marketing messages to the right people at the right time for free or at a reasonable fee. Social media allows brands to discover more about their audience's demographic, geographic, and personal details. This information will enable organizations to tailor their messaging and boost their content engagement.

There are five fundamental pillars on which social media marketing stands, including:

- Social Strategy
- Planning and Publishing
- Listening and Engagement
- Analytics and Reporting
- Advertising

1. SOCIAL STRATEGY

It is not advisable to publish something on social media without stepping back and looking at the bigger picture. In this sense, one must first consider their social media strategy. You will need to answer several questions to help develop your social media marketing strategy, including:

What are your social media goals?

A social media goal is a statement about what your brand intends to achieve using a particular social marketing strategy or the entire strategy. How do you want to use social media to help you reach your business goals?

Some businesses want to use social media to increase brand awareness, while others want to use it to boost traffic and sales on their website. Furthermore, companies can use social media to generate engagement around their brands, create a community or use it as one of their customer support channels for their clients.

The goals you set can apply to a single ad, organic post, or the whole social media campaign. By the way, why are social media goals important? If you can formulate proper social media marketing goals, they will help you to:

- structure and simplify your workflow,
- manage your social media marketing budget,
- verify your marketing return on investment,
- and line up your brand's social media activity with its broader business objectives.

Also, your goals should reflect your brand's specific business needs. Here are examples of social media marketing goals you can draw inspiration from:

- **Enhance brand awareness:** this means increasing the number of people who are acquainted with your brand. It is an ideal goal for organizations launching a new product and trying to break into the market. You'll learn in Chapter 9 how to measure brand awareness on social media using specific metrics.
- **Manage brand status:** social media marketing is a popular tool that brands use to establish trust. Nowadays, trust contributes to brand growth. You can use this objective to measure public attitude towards your brand.
- **Boost traffic to your website:** remember, you should not limit your social media marketing goals to actions that take place on social

media platforms only. Your company's website is a critical component of your social media strategy.

- **Improve engagement with your community:** engagement refers to any visible interaction with your brand on social media. Examples of engagement include comments, likes, and shares in your post. While some consider engagement a vanity metric, that is not entirely true. Brands can use these softer signals to track how well their content meets the target audience's needs.
- **Improve conversions and sales:** Conversion refers to when a user takes action on your website or social media posts. The action could be registering for a webinar, signing up for a newsletter, or purchasing. This is an important goal for brands whose social media presence is not translating into sales.
- **Generate leads:** not all social media interactions usually result in sales. Don't fret; that is okay! Suppose you want to fill your funnel with prospective clients. Your goal is to then generate more social leads. Such campaigns typically yield any information that can help you follow up with a social media user. Leads are a type of conversion; hence the two goals work well in similar situations.
- **Deliver customer service:** you can use your social media presence to keep the customers you already have. This goal could take different forms, such as reducing wait times, enhancing customer satisfaction, and establishing a new customer service channel.
- **Improve business social listening:** if your priority is to find out what you need to know, this is a worthy goal. There are two steps involved in social listening: first, examine social media activity applicable to your brand. After that, analyze the information you gather for insights about your organization or industry.

Finally, your social media goals should be **SMART**:

- **Specific**: they should state precisely what you intend to achieve. Be as precise as possible. For example, to increase the number of followers on LinkedIn.
- **Measurable:** you should have specific metrics to define success. At this point, you can add numbers to the previous example, i.e., double the number of followers on LinkedIn.

- **Attainable:** while it is tempting to aim high, it is best not to set yourself up for failure. You cannot reach a million dollars in sales by next week if you have just launched. Right? Therefore, based on our example above, check your account's growth performance in the previous months. Ensure that your historical performance aligns with your goals.
- **Relevant:** the goal should fit the brand's broader plan. Every goal you set should prop up your business objectives.
- **Time-bound:** your goal should have a due date. To ensure you achieve your social media goals, please have a timeline for completion. For example, you can double your LinkedIn followers within four months.

WHICH SOCIAL MEDIA PLATFORMS WILL YOU USE?

There are about 200 social media platforms you can choose from. So, how do you determine which one is best for your case? Below are six tips to guide you on how to pick the ideal channels for your business. However, it would help if you choose one channel, set it up, and run it successfully before you go for the next one. Launching multiple channels simultaneously could back-fire on you.

Consider your audience first

Your audience is critical when selecting a social media platform. Nothing else is essential if your target audience is not active on your chosen channel. Be that as it may, an average Internet user is said to have around eight social media accounts. Therefore, consider other factors before you determine the best channel for your course.

Consider your brand

You must also consider your products and services, brand personality, and type of business. If your brand is highly visual, like artists and graphic designers, you might want to go for channels like Instagram or DeviantArt. If it is a B2B enterprise, then LinkedIn should be top of your list. However, the choices are not black and white. Just ensure the one you pick is fit for the purpose.

Research competitors and others in your sector

While conducting your competitive analysis, check what platforms your competitors are using, what is working, and what is not. Also, check how engaged users are on different channels.

This **channel should align with your social media marketing goals**

The reason your brand is on social media will also influence your decision. Some networks suit brands that want to share content and engage with followers. Others are best suited for enhancing customer care.

Understand the different social media platforms and their uses

Every social media platform comes with its own personality and communication methods. For example, Twitter is excellent for conversations and trending topics, while LinkedIn works best for brands that want to share professional expertise and company details. You'll learn more about the "big five" social media platforms and their uses in Chapter 4.

Consider available resources

Managing your brand's social media activity requires commitment. Your social media platforms ought to be tended, nurtured, and given what we want to return to us! Therefore, your strategy should consider the human resources available to manage your channels.

WHAT TYPE OF CONTENT WILL YOU BE SHARING?

You need to consider the type of content that will attract your audience. For example, do they like links, videos, or images? Also, determine whether the content you share is educational or entertaining. It is advisable to begin by creating a marketing persona to help you answer these questions. Remember, your answers do not have to be fixed forever; you are allowed to continually adjust your strategy as per the performance of your social media posts. Chapter 5 covers content strategy in-depth.

2. PLANNING AND PUBLISHING

An excellent social media marketing plan starts with ensuring you have a consistent presence on social media. Your continual presence on social media ensures that your brand is discovered by prospective customers from 3 billion social media users globally.

You should clearly define your channel strategy that outlines exactly where you will be publishing content. This means your marketing team should know the social media platforms where you will post the content.

Publishing on social media is straightforward. You can share a blog post, video, or image on social media platforms. However, you must plan your content beforehand and avoid creating and publishing your content sponta- neously. You should also ensure that you post top-quality content that would appeal to your target audience to maximize your reach. Furthermore, you need to post at the right frequency and timing.

Fortunately, several social media scheduling tools can enable you to publish your content automatically at your preferred time. This approach saves time and allows you to reach your target audience when they are most likely to interact with the content.

You still need an elaborate publishing calendar that includes details such as:

- Publish date
- Title/Description
- Status
- Due date
- Content type
- Producer/designer
- Editor

Once you outline the what, where, and when you are ready to start creating supporting content for publishing.

3. LISTENING AND ENGAGEMENT

Your online presence will grow as your business and social media following grows. Moreover, conversations about your brand will increase. For example, there will be more people commenting on your social media posts, messaging you directly, and tagging your brand on their social media posts.

These engagements will help establish you as an opinion leader and reliable resource in your sector. You will make your audience feel safe when you are more open and use social media to support customers. Generally, it takes about eight steps before a prospective client purchases from your business (Knight, 2017). Therefore, think of strategies you can use to shorten this process.

Remember, not all that talk about your brand on social media will let you know. Therefore, ensure you monitor social media conversations about your business. For instance, you can delight users with a positive comment or support and correct any issues before they worsen.

While you can monitor notifications on all social media platforms manually, this might not be an efficient approach. For example, you might have missed posts that did not tag your brand's social media platform. Consider using social media listening and engagement tools that will aggregate all your brand's social media mentions and messages.

4. ANALYTICS AND REPORTING

It is critical to note that you must monitor how your SMM plan is performing. For example, you need to check whether your social media reach is growing, the number of positive comments you received, and the number of people who used your hashtag on their social media posts.

Fortunately, social media platforms will provide you with this information at a basic level. For more in-depth analytics, a wide range of social media analytics tools can do that. Several parameters will help you to measure your progress on different platforms, as indicated later in Chapter 9.

5. ADVERTISING

Social media advertising is digital marketing that uses social networks like Instagram, Twitter, and Facebook to deliver paid adverts to target audiences.

Consider social media advertising if you have more funds to boost your social media marketing. Social media ads enable brands to reach a wider audience beyond those following them. These platforms have grown to the extent that you can spell out precisely to whom your ads will be displayed.

Social media platforms allow you to create target audiences using parameters such as behavior, interests, and demographics. Suppose you are running multiple social media advertising campaigns; you can use a social media advertising tool to make bulk changes, optimize your ads and automate processes.

TYPES OF SOCIAL MEDIA ADS

Since the Internet and content marketing are highly dynamic, you can use different methods in your advertising. Examples of adverts you can consider are:

Static image adverts

Photos are a popular way of social media advertising because they allow brands to show their products and services in a visually attractive manner. People online are more attracted to visuals than text and are likely to be drawn to photo ads. You can include a "Shop Now" button that redirects your customers to your website to make "check out" effortless. However, please use top-quality pictures and keep them consistent with your organic content.

Video adverts

Video ads are ideal for displaying visually appealing content. But most people on social media will only watch short-form video ads, meaning you have restricted time to keep your audience interested in your videos. Platforms such as Instagram and Facebook allow users to create short videos (reels) that users can view and interact with while going through their feeds.

Story adverts

Top-rated social media platforms like Twitter, LinkedIn, Facebook, and Instagram allow users to provide stories and ads in the form of photos and videos. The ads are usually full-screen and are displayed for a limited time, depending on the ad type and platform.

For example, if you use a photo in a Facebook story, your audience can view it for six seconds, while videos play for 15 seconds. The stories allow users to swipe to access the advertiser's website. Stories are only available for 24 hours which you can take advantage of when running short-lived promotions like deals on products or services.

Messenger adverts

These are Facebook adverts that you place in the Chats tab in Messenger. They form part of a 1:1 conversation with your client. You can use them to start automated conversations with prospective clients, answer questions directly or link the user to your website.

Carousel adverts

Carousel adverts are ideal for showcasing different features of a product. You can also use this type of ad to explain the step-by-step process. Do you have several products and services? A carousel advert will help you present them.

Use different elements of your carousel ad to present a more compelling message or story. Please ensure you opt out of the automatic optimization feature if you want them to remain in a particular order.

Slideshow adverts

A slideshow is an ad that combines multiple static images to create a video. You can use slideshows if you don't have video-specific resources to generate videos. Furthermore, consider using stock photos if you don't have professional photography available.

Collection adverts

Collection adverts allow you to highlight your products in your Facebook feed. The ad has a cover photo or video and four smaller product images with their prices, among other details. Consider it your digital storefront or an instant glance into your catalog. This ad format makes it effortless for viewers to learn more about your product without leaving Facebook.

TIPS FOR DESIGNING SOCIAL ADS

1. Don't overuse filters!
2. Ensure all image elements are legible. Don't use overlapped logos and text covering all the essential parts of the background image.
3. If your goal is to reach maximum visibility, consider using unique photos with strong contrasts and attractive colors.
4. Suppose you are offering discounts; please include them in the image. Use colors associated with sales—for instance, red for the previous price and green for the reduced price.
5. If your ads' objectives are installations, registrations, or purchases, use designs optimized for conversions.

DIGITAL MARKETING SALES FUNNEL

In the digital marketing sector, the sales funnel is among the core concepts which can transform your business significantly. If you want to take your business from grass to grace, you must learn all the fundamentals of a sales funnel.

WHAT IS A SALES FUNNEL?

Picture the real-world funnel. When you pour a substance at the top, it all filters towards one point. The same thing happens in marketing. For example, the people who come across your business are at the top of your sales funnel. But unlike the real-world funnel, not all filter down to the end. Many usually leave the funnel without making purchases.

Luckily, if you optimize your sales funnel fittingly, there will be more people completing your sales funnel because it serves your prospective clients appropriately. With that in mind, you can define a *sales funnel* as the journey a customer or potential customer goes through from discovering your business to when they are ready to purchase.

Obviously, they will take specific steps along the way. In digital marketing terms, these steps are referred to as the "top," "middle," and "bottom" of the funnel.

WHY A SALES FUNNEL IS ESSENTIAL FOR YOUR BUSINESS

One of the objectives businesses spend millions on their marketing ventures is to drive sales. To achieve this, they usually rely on a sales funnel that shows the path their prospective clients take. Here are the three primary reasons why you should create a sales funnel for your business:

It helps to generate new leads and build relationships methodically

Believe it or not, many business owners depend on hope marketing. Are you one of them? Hope marketing simply means waiting around for word of mouth or talking to people randomly, hoping they will be interested in your business. But they don't ask anyone to take action or pay them.

As a result, they fail because they lack elaborate plans to drive leads and build relationships with the right prospects. Fortunately, a sales funnel can help businesses generate new leads in an economical and timely manner.

Building a sales funnel allows you to determine who will be at the top, middle and bottom. This knowledge will enable you to deliver appropriate messages to these prospects based on their position in the funnel.

It helps turn cold leads into paying clients

Sales funnels will help your business turn cold leads into a more receptive audience and paying clients. It is an effective strategy because it gives your sales team critical insights into your prospects' thought processes, challenges, problems, and decisions. In fact, nearly 80 percent of marketing leads are not turned into paying customers because businesses don't have a system that tells them what their prospects are thinking at every stage of the purchasing journey.

It helps deliver the right message at the right time

One notable mistake many businesses make is to create one message for everyone in their audience. Suppose you have two prospects: one is a first-time visitor to your website who interacted with your content. The second is a prospect that has contacted you asking for more details about your business.

Would it be effective if you delivered the same message to these two prospects? I don't think so! This is where the sales funnel comes in handy. It will enable you to convey the right message to the right people at the right moment. The best sales teams usually target prospective customers' needs at a particular stage and deliver the message accordingly.

HOW DOES THE SALES FUNNEL WORK?

Every business uses a unique approach to manage sales and customer touch-points. Nonetheless, a sales funnel can be structured into four different stages that cut across:

- Awareness
- Interest
- Decision
- Purchase/action

Stage One: Awareness/Discovery

In this phase, your ideal customer may discover they have a challenge. However, they are still struggling to identify what it is. They have many questions concerning their problem and how your business can help. So, they are looking for information to educate them about the problem.

Here, you need content about your products or services that your prospects can access from your website or social media platforms. If you sell mattresses, your prospective client is probably asking why they wake up with lower back pain at this point.

Therefore, at the top of the funnel, your prospects need the information to help them articulate their problems and ask the correct questions. Your job at this phase is to create content that can educate your prospects on their problems. This will enable you to convert new prospects into leads, moving them a step down the funnel.

Content Ideas

Blogging

Blogging is an excellent way to create awareness and interest in your products or brand. People who read your blogs provide traffic to your website. Therefore, use blogs to create awareness and ensure you use the right keywords to attract the right visitors using organic channels. Start by identifying your prospects' problems and pains and create blog posts around them. Alternatively, write on blog topics your audience wants to discover. Promote your blog on different platforms, including social media.

Social Media Posts

Your social media platforms play an essential role at this stage. More and more people are turning to social media to look for information on different subjects, such as customer reviews and branded content. You'll discover more later in this book on how to create content for different social media platforms.

How-To Videos

This is another excellent method you can use to inform people about a problem and offer a step-by-step solution. You can use videos at all stages of your sales funnel. YouTube is arguably the ideal channel for delivering how-to videos. Please ensure you optimize your content for the target keywords to reach the correct audience. You can also use videos in your website content and blogs.

Webinars

This approach allows you to deliver information using videos and live video streaming. Different social media platforms allow you to go live. Take advantage of these features to create awareness of your brand, products, and services.

Stage Two: Interest

Your prospects now understand their problems and know something about your brand. However, they still want to learn more even though they are not ready to buy. They are still exploring possible solutions. Note that they are looking for solution types and are not evaluating the solution. Here, you must provide content that informs them how your mattress can help them get rid of back pain. It would help if you also told them why they should buy your product.

Stage Three: Decision

During this phase, your prospective clients will be ready to make a purchase. Remember, they could also be considering your competitors. Furthermore, they are at the bottom of the funnel and understand their problem and possible solutions.

More importantly, they have the details to choose the business to buy the solution. They are asking themselves vendor-driven questions; therefore, you should present your best offers. You can include small factors like a bonus product, free shipping, or discounts to differentiate yourself from your competitors. Ensure you make your offers very attractive, so your target audience will rush to join your client list.

Content Ideas

Case Studies

Case studies help to show your ideal customers the results you've gotten for your current customers. It can create dramatic results because a good case study offers quantitative data and comprehensive details on how a brand solves a problem. Showcasing your success stories to potential customers is an excellent way to generate interest in your products and services.

Product Comparisons

People look at product pros and cons to help them decide. Therefore it is an excellent idea to compare your products or services to those offered by your competitors to show your solutions are better.

Lead Magnets

Lead magnets are an ideal way of generating interest in your brand. You can grow your email list by offering something valuable, such as an eBook or free initial consultation.

Stage Four: Action

At the bottom of your business sales funnel, your potential customers take action. They buy your products or services, and you manage to convert a cold lead into a client through an elaborate process. Here, explore how to turn one purchase into six or ten.

If they don't do business with you, don't despair! Your efforts can still bear fruit. Develop nurture campaigns to remain top of your potential clients' minds. Also, ensure you have a remarketing and lookalike audience to return to your potential customers one more time.

You can also engage with them and persuade them to leave feedback. You can add another level to your funnel to deal with customer retention. The story should not end once someone makes a purchase. You should work on turning a customer into a repeat customer and brand ambassador.

Content Ideas

Free Trial

At this stage, your prospective customer may want to buy your mattress, but they don't know which one would be perfect. Therefore, you can offer them a free mattress trial to help them decide. Alternatively, you can produce guides to help prospects select the right mattress. Car dealers offer a "test drive" approach to help clients decide faster. Offer something similar to your prospects.

Consultation Offer

If you are about to close a sale, you need to offer your prospects some motivation. The motivation could come in the form of a demo or free consultation. But before you create any content, ensure you learn as much as possible about your audience. It will help if your content meets the person at the stage they are at in the sales funnel.

BUILDING A SALES FUNNEL FOR YOUR BUSINESS

By now, you have every detail to build a sales funnel for your brand. Here are some simple steps to get it done efficiently:

1. **Create a landing page:** It is advisable to build a landing page to help you in your content marketing efforts. This will help drive traffic to your brand's website. Focus on capturing leads instead of pushing people to buy your products and services. Use a landing page as a vehicle to carry your audience through the different stages. You need a clear call-to-action telling your audience what they need to do next.
2. **Create buyer personas:** Don't use guesswork and assumptions to determine who your ideal customer is. Use data and research to develop buyer personas for your business.
3. **Offer value:** you need to show your audience why they should listen to you and do what you want them to do. Developing discounts and incentives is an excellent way of creating interest. You have to give them a reason why they should proceed to the next stage.
4. **Nurture:** You've already put in a lot of effort to generate leads. It is even more important to nurture your prospects with relevant content.
5. **Call-To-Action/Upsell:** have a definitive call-to-action for each stage of your sales funnel. Ensure you upsell once your customers have made a purchase.
6. **Stay top of mind:** you must ensure you nurture relationships whether your prospects complete the funnel or not. This helps in customer retention and enables you to remain on top of their minds for some time.

OPTIMIZING YOUR SALES FUNNEL

- Use the right message to the right people at the right time (#R3MAT). People's needs change as they move down the sales funnel. Use the

#R3MAT approach to convey the right message in the right state of your sales funnel.

- Use CRM: Use CRM to streamline your sales and marketing processes.
- Use social proof: social proof helps to increase your conversion rate. Social proof from your current clients and reliable industry experts will significantly help.
- Identify any cracks in your sales funnel: suppose something is not effective, try something different.
- View relevant data: track your performance. Start by setting realistic goals and measure your performance against those goals.

Pro Tip: A sales funnel is a journey that starts with your prospect discovering your business, discovering more about it, and deciding the product they should buy before making a purchase. Your secret is to clearly define this journey and develop a strategy to move people through these stages.

KEY TAKEAWAYS

- There are five significant pillars on which social media marketing stands.
- Your social media strategy is the first thing you must consider before doing anything else.
- Different social media platforms are ideal for different social media strategies.

Having learned the *Fundamentals of Social Media Marketing*, it is time to see why you need social media marketing for your brand. Please read **Chapter 3: Benefits of Social Media Marketing** for more details.

CHAPTER 3
BENEFITS OF SOCIAL MEDIA MARKETING

Picture this: you spend at least six hours a week boosting your brand's recognition, traffic, and sales at little or no cost! Amazing, right? Nearly 90% of marketers have acknowledged that social media has generated massive exposure for their brands, and that is just one of its numerous advantages. Social media platforms have emerged as a critical part of every marketing strategy. Furthermore, the benefits of social media marketing are enormous and any brand not implementing this cost-effective strategy is missing out on an extraordinary marketing opportunity.

You can easily see the importance of social media marketing in marketing, and many marketers have achieved business growth using different platforms. So, how does social media marketing benefit your business?

DRIVE TRAFFIC

Businesses that don't market their brands on social media limit their inbound traffic to their usual customers. This is because the people acquainted with your business are more likely to search for similar keywords that you already rank for. As a result, if you don't use social media as part of your marketing strategy, it will be more challenging to reach anyone outside your current client circle.

Every social media profile you include in your marketing plan acts as a gateway to your website. Moreover, every content you share on the platforms is an opportunity to get a new client. Social media attracts people from diverse backgrounds and behaviors. This means that brands will be interacting with an audience having different needs and different schools of thought.

In this sense, brands must organize their content on multiple platforms to allow different individuals to reach their business organically. For example, older people might search for your website using a specific keyword on Facebook. However, millennials will likely use different social media platforms because they search for products differently. Marketing on social media allows you to open up your business to broader and more versatile consumers worldwide.

GENERATE LEADS AND CUSTOMERS

Increased visibility enables your business to gain more opportunities for conversion. Every blog post, comment, video, or photo may lead viewers to your organization's website and boost traffic. Social media marketing allows your brand to give a positive impression using a humanization factor. The brand personifies itself by sharing content, posting statuses, and commenting on social media. People want to do business with people, not organizations.

Reviews from marketers revealed that taking time to create a good relationship with consumers generated positive results in sales. Therefore, a visitor is more likely to think about your business when they need your products and services if you give an excellent first impression. Social media offers a higher lead-to-close rate than outbound marketing.

If your brand is interactive online, consumers following your brand's social media accounts can begin to trust the credibility of your business. Many social media users use the platforms to stay connected with their families, friends, and communities. Therefore, if you throw yourself in the mix, they will likely mention your brand to a family member when they need your products or services. Such a referral offers your business top-quality social proof.

INCREASE BRAND AWARENESS

Social media is undoubtedly a cost-effective digital marketing method brands use to organize content and boost their business visibility. Therefore, implementing a social media strategy will increase your brand recognition because you will be engaging with a wide range of consumers. To get this benefit, you must take your time to create a social media profile for your business. After that, ensure you hire employees, business partners, and sponsors to interact with your content through sharing, commenting, and liking.

When people interact with your content, they boost your brand awareness which helps build your reputation as a business. Every post you share will be introduced to a new group of individuals, which could lead them to become prospective clients. The more people know about your brand, the merrier!

Reports suggest that over 91% of marketers invested a few hours weekly in social media marketing, which significantly boosted their brand exposure (Media, 2022). It is evident that by simply having a social media page, your brand will benefit. Furthermore, using it regularly will help generate a wider audience for your business.

IMPROVED SEARCH ENGINE RANKINGS

While posting on social media boosts traffic to your business website, it requires more effort to register significant success. In this regard, search engine optimization (SEO) is essential to achieve higher rankings and generate traffic for your business. Chapter 6 covers SEO and Social Media Marketing in detail.

Social media does not directly increase your brand's search engine rankings. Industry experts claim that marketers who have been using social media for a while have seen improved search engine rankings. If your brand can rank in top positions for your keywords, it will revolutionize your traffic and keep generating positive results for your brand.

Truth be told, everyone uses Google to look for information. Also, most Google users are less likely to navigate past the first page because they are likely to find the answer on page 1 of the results. Therefore, if your page does not rank at the top of search engine results, you must fine-tune your SEO strategy.

For a better chance to rank highly through social media, create high-quality content that includes your targeted keywords. Content like case studies, blogs, business information, infographics, and employee photos makes your brand's social media profile captivating and convincing.

Posting quality content allows you to build a social media community where your followers like, comment, and share your content. Above all, social media allows you to put your brand in front of industry influencers who will write about your brand and provide links back. This directly increases your search engine rankings.

ENHANCED CUSTOMER SATISFACTION

Social media is a trendy communication and networking platform. When you create a voice for your brand using these platforms, it helps to humanize your company. Customers appreciate knowing they will get a personalized response instead of automated messages when posting comments on your pages. The ability to acknowledge each comment indicates that you are attentive to your visitor's needs and want to give them the best experience.

Every time you interact with a customer on your brand's social media accounts, you demonstrate your compassion for your clients. Whether it is a complaint or a question, social media allows you to address the issue using interpersonal dialogue. A brand that devotes itself to customer satisfaction takes time to compose personal messages. Such a brand will be viewed in a positive light even if it is responding to a client complaint.

IMPROVED BRAND LOYALTY

Every brand aims to develop a loyal customer base. Bearing in mind that customer satisfaction goes in tandem with brand loyalty, it is critical to engage your customers regularly and develop a bond with them. Therefore, don't limit your social media activities to introducing products and holding promotional campaigns. Your customers consider these platforms service channels where they can communicate directly with your business.

The millennial generation is regarded as the most brand loyal customer. It is also evident that customers are more faithful to the brands that engage with them on social media platforms. Because tech-savvy millennials require communication with their brands, businesses need to run proper social media marketing to get the attention of their most influential consumers.

BRAND AUTHORITY

Your business becomes more authoritative when you achieve customer satisfaction and brand loyalty. However, all these factors come down to how you communicate. When consumers see your brand posting on social media, especially replies to consumer concerns and original content, it gives them the impression that you are more reliable.

Therefore, ensure you communicate with your customers regularly to demonstrate that your business takes customer satisfaction seriously. Satisfied clients are usually eager to spread the word about a great product or service and often turn to social media to express their delight. When customers mention your brand on social media, they advertise your business and show new visitors your value, boosting your brand authority. Once you get several satisfied customers who are vocal about their positive experiences, you can allow actual customers to advertise your products and services.

ALLOWS YOU TO LEARN FROM COMPETITORS

Social media is an excellent way to keep tabs on your competitors. By following their social media activities, you can analyze their social media strategy, their products, and the campaigns they are running. You can also monitor their level of interaction with followers.

Such an analysis allows you to examine what is and is not working for your competitors. Consequently, you will determine how to adjust your brand's approach to beat the competition. Also, reviewing your competitor's social media accounts allows you to ensure your marketing stands out and is unique to your business.

SOCIAL MEDIA MARKETING IS COST-EFFECTIVE

Social media marketing is undoubtedly the most cost-effective and diverse method of promoting your brand. For example, creating a profile on most social media platforms does not cost anything. You can also run a paid campaign to boost your content. Still, the cost is reasonably low compared to other advertising platforms.

Therefore, if you run your social media marketing well, you boost your chances of producing more significant returns on your investment. If your current social media marketing strategy includes paid advertising, ensure you start small and gradually work your way up as you become more experienced. Moreover, social media lets you track your performance and adjust your strategy from real-time data.

GET MARKETPLACE INSIGHTS

One of the most valuable benefits of social media is marketplace insight. The platform allows you to meet your customers' needs and thoughts by directly talking with them. Also, you can discover your customers' interests and opinions by monitoring activity on your profiles. It can be challenging to gain such insights if your business does not have a social media presence.

Furthermore, using social media as a complementary research tool allows you to gain information that will help you understand your industry better. After getting a massive following, you can use additional tools to evaluate your consumers' demographics.

Another insightful aspect of social media marketing is that it allows you to segment your content management lists based on topic and identify the content types that generate the most impressions. These tools enable your brand to measure conversions based on posts on social media platforms to find the ideal combination for generating income.

BOOST SALES

The aim of posting polls, videos, updates, and surveys daily is to engage customers and personalize your brand. Industry experts argue that building relationships with current and prospective buyers results in steady sales. A business with a solid online presence offers interesting content that triggers interaction and gives users a reason to come back. Also, when your consumers feel valued and heard, they are likely to refer their friends and family, which in turn boosts your sales.

KEY TAKEAWAYS

- There are many benefits associated with social media marketing.
- The benefits your brand will get depend on your strategy.
- If a brand strives to ensure they achieve brand loyalty and customer satisfaction, it will benefit from social proof.
- To benefit from paid promotions on social media platforms, start with a small budget and gradually increase.

As you can see, the benefits of using social media marketing are many. However, you will not register these benefits without having a proper social media marketing plan. One thing that ensures you have an effective strategy is understanding your social media platforms. Please read the next chapter to learn more about *"The Big Eight"* social media platforms and how you can use them effectively.

CHAPTER 4
EIGHT BEST SOCIAL MEDIA MARKETING PLATFORMS

Social media platforms provide the most effective marketing channels for businesses. They are an excellent way to build your brand's awareness, connect with current customers and generate new leads to fill your funnel.

However, there are more than 65 social media platforms. It's hard to choose. This chapter will help you with that as it discusses the top 8 social media platforms for your business. Furthermore, it teaches you how to use the platforms to help your brand achieve its goals.

It is essential to remember that the platforms discussed here are not the silver bullet solution to your marketing woes. This section just teaches you how to use the platforms for growth, and then you can choose what works best for your current situation. Nevertheless, as a general rule of thumb, go for a platform that works best for your current situation and grows gradually.

FACEBOOK MARKETING

Facebook is undoubtedly the largest social media platform worldwide. It is also one of the biggest local business directories available. The platform attracts users from different age groups who use it to communicate with family and friends. Facebook users also use it to participate in group forums, follow brands and find businesses in their locality.

This social media platform can work for any industry. However, studies have shown that beauty and fitness, jobs and education, and employment and job training experience the highest conversion rates. Conversely, healthcare, finance, and restaurants get the highest engagement rates on Facebook.

To use Facebook for marketing, you need a Business Facebook Page. Take your time to create an effective Page to start on the right note.

How to create a Facebook Business Page

The majority of Facebook contains professional profiles. However, as a business aspiring to establish its presence on the social network, you need to create a Page. Your Facebook Page is Facebook's equivalent of your business profile. Pages are similar to profile pages but contain more specific information applicable to your business or organization and its cause.

People will connect with your business page by "liking" it and becoming a fan. Facebook will likely shut down your Page if you create a personal profile from page to Page. Follow these steps to create a Facebook Page:

1. Create Your Facebook Page

To create your Page, go to https://www.facebook.com/pages/create/. While there, you will have two categories to select from:

- Business or Brand
- Community or Public Figure

Facebook offers these two options to allow you to customize the fields of the Page better. For this section, let's select a "Business or Brand." You can input your **Page Name** and **Category**. It is essential to choose the name wisely. This is because changing the name later will be a tedious process.

At this point, Facebook will prompt you to log into your Facebook account if you haven't. However, your personal details will not appear on the Page unless you add them. Press "**Get Started,**" and Facebook will automatically redirect you to add a **Profile Photo** and a **Cover Photo** for the new Page. You can skip this step and do it later.

2. Add Photos

Profile Picture: A profile picture is the first step to giving your Facebook Page an identity. It is your page's primary visual will appear in search results, alongside your content that appears in a user's newsfeed. The image should be square, at least 180 x 180 pixels. This is your first impression so use a recognizable image like your logo. If you are a restaurant, you can use the image of your most popular offering.

Cover Photo: A cover photo is a large, horizontal image that spans the top of the page. This photo expresses your Page's identity, and you can update it based on seasons, campaigns, and offerings. Your ideal cover photo should be 851 x 315 pixels.

3. Add a Short Description

This will help you communicate to your audience what your business is all about. Click on the "Add a Short Description" to complete this process. Facebook allows you to use up to 255 characters to create a description. This description appears in search results and on your Page. In this sense, you should ensure it is descriptive and concise. However, that does not mean you shy away from showing your brand's personality.

4. Create a Username

This is the last step on the welcome menu. Your username appears in your custom Facebook URL also called a vanity URL. It makes it effortless for people to remember your Page. You have 50 characters to create a unique name.

5. Add Page Shortcuts

There are several other things you can do to customize your Page. For example, you can add your Page as a shortcut to your newsfeed for easy access. Go to your newsfeed, click on "Edit" next to "Shortcuts" in the left vertical navigation to make it effortless to navigate to your Page.

6. Set up Page Roles

Facebook allows multiple people from your business to edit and post from the Page without sharing their login credentials. Designate who has what level of editing access by creating page roles. Locate "Settings" on the top navigation bar, and click on "Page Roles" in the left navigation bar. Here are the few options you have:

- **Admin:** Admins can manage all aspects of the business page. They have all the rights like the page creator. Therefore, assign this role wisely. Admins can do the following:

  - Send messages

  - Publish as the Page

  - Create ads

  - Respond or delete comments

  - Assign page roles

- **Editor:** Editors have equal access to Admins. The only difference is that they can't assign page roles.
- **Moderator:** Moderators cannot publish as the Page but can send messages, respond to and delete comments. They can also create ads.
- **Advertiser:** Advertisers can create ads and view insights.
- **Analyst:** As an analyst, you don't have any publishing rights. However, you can see which admin published a particular post and insights.
- **Jobs Manager:** Jobs managers can do all the Advertiser's jobs. They can also publish and manage jobs.

7. Customize Your Notifications

You'll find the "Notifications" tab in the settings menu. From there, you can customize how you will receive alerts for activity on your Page. For instance, you can choose to receive a notification each time there is an activity or get one notification after 12 or 24 hours.

8. Add a Page CTA

A Facebook Page allows your business to attract an audience you wouldn't have reached with a traditional website. Facebook introduced a call-to-action button in 2014. Click "+Add a Button" beneath your cover photo to create a

CTA. There are multiple choices to select from based on what you want. For instance, do you want to view a service, get in touch, make a donation or purchase, learn more or download an app.

9. Organize Your Page Tabs

You can tailor your Page's tabs to the content users see when they visit your Page. For example, you can give visitors options such as browsing photos, visiting your Pinterest account, seeing open jobs, or finding a store near you. If you want to change the tabs, go to "Settings" > "Templates and Tabs." You can use Facebook's default tabs or add yours.

10. Verify Your Page

You could be eligible for a verification badge based on how you categorized your Page. A blue badge shows that Facebook has confirmed the authenticity of the Page for a public figure, brand, or media company. A gray badge means Facebook has confirmed the authenticity of the business or organization page.

While a verification badge is unnecessary, it gives your Page a sense of authority. This is essential if your business is in eCommerce or offers online services and wants to build trust with prospective customers and initiate online transactions.

Before checking whether you are eligible, ensure your Page has a profile picture and cover photo. Navigate to "Settings"> "General." You will find "Page Verification" and enter your publicly listed phone number, country, and language. After that, you will receive a call with a verification code. With that, you are now ready to start your Facebook marketing.

HOW TO USE FACEBOOK AS A MARKETING TOOL

Facebook is a popular social marketing tool because of its versatility. You can use it for a wide range of social media marketing activities. Before exploring how to use Facebook for marketing, understand the Facebook Algorithm.

In the past, Facebook used to show posts in the newsfeed using a reverse-chronological order. In this sense, your most recent post appears at the top of the newsfeed. However, with many people and businesses posting on Facebook, there will be so many posts on people's newsfeed that it will be challenging to go through all the posts.

As a result, Facebook introduced a system that organizes the posts you see in your newsfeed. This is what is referred to as the Facebook Algorithm. The algorithm uses several factors to determine how relevant a post might be and shows you the most relevant posts at the top of your newsfeed. The algorithm is dynamic, but here are the fundamentals of how it works:

First, the algorithm has to look at which of the posts are most relevant to you using a relevance score. Facebook News Feed uses several factors to give all the posts a relevance score. Essential factors include:

- Who Posted
- Types of content
- Interactions with the post
- When the post was posted

Therefore, not all people who like your Facebook Page will see all your posts. On average, your Page might reach around five percent or lower of your fans. To reach more people with your Business Page, post content that your target audience would care about and interact with.

In this regard, knowing the different types of Facebook posts is advisable. The six primary post types you can use are:

- **Text:** this is the most basic type and easiest to create. But it is the least visible on the newsfeed. Therefore, it is advisable to attach multimedia to help your post stand out more.
- **Image:** you can post one or multiple images. Ensure the images you post are the right size, i.e.500 pixels in height and width.
- **Video:** is currently the most popular and most engaging format. Studies have shown that videos get twice as much engagement as other post types. Ideas for videos include explainer videos, demo videos, interviews with industry experts, event coverage, behind-the-scenes sneak peeks, webinars, and product commercial shoots.
- **Link:** These posts show a preview of the link attached. It usually has an image, a headline, and a description. You can also add text

45

together with the link.

- **Stories:** This is another popular Facebook post type. It is a vertical image or video that uses the entire screen of mobile phones. Stories usually disappear after 24 hours. You can use stories for advertisements.
- **Pinned Posts:** you can use an existing post on your Page as a "pinned post," meaning it will always be at the top of your Page. This is essential for a welcome message, customer support contacts, and links to important pages. You can change your pinned posts whenever you like.

Here is how to use Facebook for marketing:

Local Marketing

Facebook is the top-rated local business directory. Data from Statista shows that around 60% of Facebook users visit local business pages at least once weekly (Dixon, 2022). That way, you can promote your Page and use it to build relationships, update customers, and keep in touch with the local community.

Advertising

Although your Facebook business page is a popular hub for people who know your business, it is not the ideal platform for reaching new clients organically. Studies have shown that its organic reach is around 2.2%. Conversely, its size and targeting abilities have put it at par with Google as a top-rated digital advertising platform. You can reach up to 36.7% of the adult population using Facebook ads, the highest of all social media platforms (Wagner, 2021).

Additionally, the average Facebook user clicks on 12 adverts per month. The volume of impressions can boost brand awareness, improving your advertising performance elsewhere. Over six million businesses advertise on Facebook, promoting their products and services.

Facebook advertising offers the most comprehensive targeting that enables you to reach a specific audience. Some parameters you can use to specify your target audience include location, demographics, interests, and behavior.

You can also use the Facebook Ad Manager to create ads that will show on Messenger, Instagram, and Audience Network. The steps to run a Facebook ad are straightforward, as outlined below:

1. Set your objective
2. Choose your target audience
3. Decide whether you want to run your ads
4. Set your budget
5. Choose a format (photo, video, carousel, collection, or slideshow)

It might feel daunting to spend money on advertising. However, diving right in and getting started is the best way to learn. Please don't shy away from experimenting, as it will enable you to learn about post types that resonate well with your audience. You will also learn how to select the right audience and handle your budget.

Community and relationship building

Don't allow Facebook's low organic reach to stop you from using it to connect with your audience. Many people will visit your Facebook business page for announcements, sales, store closings, or other updates. If you use your Page for these purposes, your clients and close followers will be checking your Page frequently.

As a result, you won't have to put much effort into ensuring you appear in their feeds. Furthermore, you can tailor your posts to the quality of traffic by visiting your Page. For example, you can trigger discussions, engage with individuals and encourage direct messaging.

You might also want to experiment with Facebook Groups. It offers an effortless way to start an online community for the advocates of your brand. Most of your clients are likely already on Facebook, and Facebook Groups offer multiple features to help connect people better. Groups can also increase your organic reach on Facebook.

What to post

Facebook is mainly a conversational platform. But when a consumer likes your Facebook business page, it is highly likely they expect to receive updates. For example, they want to be aware of any future sales and promotions and get updates on new products or any information on upcoming events or launches.

In this sense, connecting with your followers and offering them the right content is critical. Consider sharing different content types and see which type resonates well with your followers by attracting the most impressions, engagements, and shares. Once you discover the content type your audience responds to, keep using that type to share.

How often to share

There is no limit to the number of times you can share on your Facebook business page. However, dominating your audience's feeds is a social media blunder you should avoid. Studies have revealed that engagement rates per post reduce significantly for businesses that post more than twice a day and those that post only once weekly.

Therefore, posting too much might cause people to unfollow your Page, while posting too little will hurt your engagement metrics. Consider the amount of content you have to promote and post appropriately. The proper strategy would be to have one update per day.

Host Facebook Contests

Facebook contests, promotions, and sweepstakes are excellent Facebook marketing approaches that can boost brand awareness. However, it is critical to note that you can't host contests through Facebook. In this sense, you have to use a third-party app to create your Facebook contest and direct users to the app from your Facebook page.

HOW BRANDS ARE USING FACEBOOK TODAY

Facebook Shops

Facebook introduced Facebook Shops in 2020. Many businesses globally turned to this new feature as their official method of selling on the platform. As a result, the number of Facebook Shops and monthly global users has increased significantly.

Live Shopping

Consumers were demanding a more interactive platform, and Facebook's answer was Live Shopping. This interactive feature also enables businesses to show their products in action. Reports have shown that Facebook is the second most popular platform worldwide for Live Shopping. Additionally, Live Shopping gives brands massive authenticity points.

For instance, it allows them to put faces to their brands, making them more likely to capture the attention of scrollers. Furthermore, humanizing your account is an excellent thing. It also allows you to be more transparent and vulnerable, which boosts sales of your products.

Messenger for Customer Service

Consumers no longer click "Contact Us." Instead, the modern-day consumer wants quick communication through social media platforms. Studies have shown that consumers feel more confident when they receive a message from a business.

INSTAGRAM MARKETING

Instagram has over two billion active users, making it an ideal social media marketing platform (Martin, 2022). The platform has shaped the landscape of social commerce and the creator economy. Additionally, it has transformed how brands use social media. In this section, you will discover how you can use Instagram marketing to take your brand to greater heights.

WHAT IS INSTAGRAM MARKETING?

Instagram marketing involves using Instagram to grow your brand aware-ness, leads, audience, and sales. It has emerged as an effective marketing platform for brands that target people aged between 16 and 34. Before we look at Instagram marketing strategies, let's look at how to set up Instagram for marketing.

HOW TO SET UP AN INSTAGRAM BUSINESS PROFILE

You need an Instagram Business account for the marketing tips you'll learn here to work. Fortunately, it is free to create. Alternatively, you can convert your existing Personal account to a Business account. Therefore, if you have a personal account, please skip to Step 3.

Before setting up a business profile on Instagram, it is best to have a Facebook Page. Fortunately, you know how to set up a Facebook Page. Once your Facebook profile is ready, you can connect it to your Instagram business profile.

Here is how to create an Instagram Business Profile:

Step 1: Download Instagram

You need an Instagram app to create a profile. It is available on iOS and Android, so you can download it from the App Store or Google Play Store.

Step 2: Create a Personal Account

Click "Create new account" and follow the prompts. Enter your email and phone number, and choose a username and password. You don't have to fill out the entire profile at this point. You will learn later how to optimize your profile.

Step 3: Switch your Personal account to a Business account

Open the menu from your profile and go to Settings. Select Switch to a professional account and choose Business as the account type. After that, follow the prompts to convert the account.

At this point, you can also click on "Switch to Business Profile" then "Continue" to connect to Facebook. If your profile is set to private, it might not be possible to switch the account. Therefore, ensure that you change your profile to public.

Click on "Continue As" to connect to the Facebook Page. Suppose your Facebook Page is not visible; check whether you're listed as an admin in the settings menu.

Get Verified

While not all top companies are verified, studies have shown that over 70% of brands with a million followers or more are verified. You don't need a "verified" badge to be successful on Instagram. However, having it can help you earn trust and stand out from your competitors.

HOW TO OPTIMIZE YOUR INSTAGRAM PROFILE

Your Instagram profile is a critical reflection of your brand. This is why you should spend time planning your profile's overall look. Your brand has a few seconds to convert someone who lands on your page into a follower. Here is how to optimize your Instagram page:

Create a consistent Instagram aesthetic

One critical aspect of creating your Instagram feed is ensuring your photos look great beside each other. So examine your Instagram feed before posting a photo to see how your images fit together. Here are some great tips:

- **Pick a color scheme:** your Instagram feed should have a consistent color scheme. This implies that all the colors of your feed should fit together seamlessly. Please choose a color palette and incorporate it into your branding consistently.
- **Focus on lighting:** Lighting is critical for aesthetics and curation. The lighting and color choices tie everything together regardless of the subject matter.
- **Space out your content:** knowing where you will put every photo and how you'll plan your content to fit together is essential. Your objective should be to create a depth of field. For instance, space out busy photos and blend them with minimal photos to get an excellent balance.
- **Keep things consistent:** for your feed to flow naturally, ensure you use a consistent approach to edit your photos. Which do you prefer? Warmer tones or cooler-toned images? Regardless of your editing style, ensure consistency so your posts align with your feed.
- **Curate user-generated feed:** you can gain a lot from your Instagram strategy if you harness the power of user-generated content.

However, ensure the photos you choose to repost align with your aesthetic and theme. Therefore, select photos that will naturally fit within your feed.

TYPES OF INSTAGRAM POSTS

You are ready to start posting amazing content with your optimized Instagram account. Instagram allows brands to post multiple content types. Here are the different types and best practices for Instagram posts.

Images

Images are the most shared posts on Instagram. It will help if you share a variety of photos to show that your brand is diverse. Moreover, Instagram followers are looking for genuine business posts instead of barefaced adverts.

Therefore, ensure you capture your brand's culture using lifestyle shots and behind-the-scenes looks. In this sense, don't post too many photos of your product. For example, if you visit Nike's Instagram page, it includes photos, most of which feature real athletes, concerts, and other types of content that promote the brand's personality.

Influencer posts

These posts use the eminence of a celebrity or famous public figures to promote a brand. Furthermore, they also include a visual of the influencer interacting with or using your product. This approach is practical because it allows you to get the attention of a different audience.

Reposts from employees

You can also get awesome content from your employees' Instagram pages as long as you ensure you tag or credit the original poster. This approach is an effortless way of curating authentic content and humanizing your business. Moreover, this will allow your followers to engage your brand and start bonding with your staff.

Motivational posts

Motivational posts usually blend simple visuals with overlaid quotes or inspiring tests. These posts can encourage your audience and magnify your brand's values. While these posts are compelling, use them sparingly so you don't look cheesy. Fortunately, some apps can help you add text to photos in a consistent manner.

Newsjacking

Nowadays, you will find holidays for everything. For instance, events like National Ice Cream Day generate a lot of engagement on social media. Your brand can join in the fun by participating in a national or global trend. A newsjacking post is an excellent way to post entertaining content related to lighthearted events.

Behind–the–scenes posts

Use these posts to give your followers a sneak peek at the parts of your business they don't usually see. It is also critical that the posts don't look staged – it is essential to be authentic!

Educational posts

Use these kinds of posts to offer your followers snackable tips on how to do or make something. Present the instructions on the photos and videos in a way that is easy to follow. For instance, several brands share tasty recipe video series that are educational, entertaining, and effortless to replicate.

User-generated content (UGC)

An excellent source of UGC is your tagged posts and posts that have your brand hashtag. Sharing photos of your fans and followers makes the original poster feel good and shows that you genuinely care about them. The best way to do this is to take a screenshot of the original post and crop it. Alternatively, you can use the reposting app.

Instagram Reels

Instagram Reels are full-screen vertical short videos. They also have several editing tools and a wide-ranging library of audio tracks. Reels also include multiple filters, video clips, stickers, interactive backgrounds, and video clips. They differ from Instagram stories, as they will not disappear after 24 hours. Moreover, the Instagram algorithm favors reels and is more likely to recommend them to people who follow you.

CREATING AN INSTAGRAM CONTENT STRATEGY

Content is critical when using Instagram for marketing. Ninety-five million photos and videos are shared on the platform daily, which attracts about 500 million people to the app. In this regard, content should form the backbone of your strategy. Having a clear vision for the type of content you want to share is essential.

Remember, there is no silver bullet solution when it comes to content strategy. Focus on creating content that aligns with your goals and audience. In this sense, you need to build your content pillars.

Building content pillars

The basis of any content strategy should be built on solid content themes or pillars. Every business, regardless of size, location or industry, has a wide range of content to share on Instagram. Examples of content pillars are:

- User-generated content
- Behind-the-scenes content
- Educational
- Product demos
- Fun/lighthearted
- Get to know the team
- Customer stories
- Team member takeovers

HOW INSTAGRAM STORIES FIT YOUR CONTENT STRATEGY

Instagram stories allow you to share photos and videos that disappear after 24 hours. Over 400 million accounts use stories daily. Stories are available in full-screen. You can enhance them using playful tools like GIFs, emojis, and stickers.

Research by Instagram discovered that people go to stories for two primary reasons:

1. To see what their friends are doing at the moment. This indicates that stories are an excellent way of bringing people closer together in real-time.
2. They also turn to stories when they want to see unfiltered, authentic content.

This offers many opportunities for brands to connect with their audiences differently. For instance, you can use stories to share your business' daily moments. You can also use stories to share user-generated content with your followers.

DEVELOPING A CONTENT PLAN

Once you have a content theme, tie everything together using a content plan. A content plan will help you define your posts' style and aesthetic feel. It will also help you decide how frequently you post on Instagram.

Style Guide

The style guide is one of the most critical parts of your social media strategy. This is essential because it ensures consistency across all your marketing channels and throughout the content you produce. Style guides contain all the necessary information for content from the beginning to the end. For Instagram posts, here are the things you should consider:

- Color palette
- Composition
- Filters
- Fonts
- Captions
- Hashtags

Composition

Composition refers to how you arrange visual elements in a work of art different from the subject of a piece. Since not all marketers are great photographers, establish some composition rules. Here are some excellent examples:

- Extra space at the top or bottom for the text
- The main focus of the picture is set to the Rule of Thirds
- Solid background color

Color palette

Pick a color palette to keep your feed consistent and focused. However, that does not mean you cannot use other colors; it just ensures your posts have a consistent and familiar feel. It would be best to keep your color palette in line with your brand's other areas.

Fonts

Suppose you'll be posting quotes or text overlays on your Instagram photos. Use consistent fonts. In this sense, choose the fonts you use on your website or other marketing materials.

Filters

Instagram filters help amateur photographers feel like professionals. Therefore, if you don't have sophisticated photography equipment and editing software, filters will help you enhance your photos. However, you should only use the filters that best represent your brand. Using a different filter for each post might make your Instagram feed feel disjointed.

Captions

Instagram restricts the captions to 2200 characters, and after three lines of text, it truncates it with an ellipsis. Captions allow you to enhance your content and many top brands use them. You can use captions to share stories or for micro-blogging. Additionally, you can use them as a snappy headline to a post or ask questions and trigger replies.

Hashtags

Hashtags are a uniform way of categorizing content on many social media platforms. It allows Instagram users to discover content and accounts worth following. Studies have shown that posts with more than 11 hashtags usually get more engagement.

INSTAGRAM ALGORITHM

Instagram replaced the chronological feed with an algorithm in 2016. The algorithm reorganizes your feeds so that you theoretically see more content relevant to you. Several factors influence how the algorithm works. Moreover, Instagram continually updates the algorithm to enhance user experience and prioritize certain content types.

Here are the factors that determine how posts perform in the Instagram algorithm:

- **Interest:** Instagram predicts how much you'll love a post. The more they think you'll love it, the higher it will appear in your feed. Your past behavior in similar posts will inform the algorithm.
- **Timeliness:** The algorithm prioritizes the most recent posts. Therefore, you are less likely to see posts from a week ago.
- **Relationship:** Brands should know when their followers are most active on Instagram. If you comment on their photos or tag your brand, Instagram assumes they are your "friends" or "family." Simply ask your audience to tag you in your posts to optimize your Instagram posts and get as many interactions as possible.
- **Frequency:** If you open your Instagram app frequently, your feed will appear more chronological because Instagram will attempt to show you the best posts since you last opened the app.
- **Following:** If you follow as many people on Instagram, the app will have more feed options.
- **Usage:** If you spend more time on Instagram, you will see more posts because the algorithm digs deeper into its catalog.

PINTEREST MARKETING

Pinterest is a powerful visual search engine and productivity tool. However, few people understand how powerful Pinterest is as a digital marketing platform. The platform offers businesses a unique way to market their brand.

Pinterest marketing uses different tactics that incorporate Pinterest into your bigger social media marketing strategy. Pinterest can help brands to:

- Reach new audiences and boost their online presence.
- Drive more traffic to their websites and online stores.
- Boost conversions such as sign-ups for newsletters, purchases, and ticket sales.

Reports suggest that nearly 80% of weekly Pinners have discovered a new brand or product on the platform. It is an ideal platform for businesses that target the same demographic that loves and uses the social media platform. For example, reports have shown that historically Pinterest has attracted women interested in shopping or starting a new project.

Recent reports from *Pinterest Business* have also shown that men and Gen Z-ers are increasingly using the platform. Pinterest has also emerged as a popular platform for people looking for positive inspiration. Before you begin promoting your business on Pinterest, you need to create an account.

HOW TO CREATE A PINTEREST BUSINESS ACCOUNT

To use Pinterest for business, ensure you have a business account, not a personal one. A business is suitable for business marketing because:

- It grants you access to analytics that help you monitor and measure the effectiveness of your Pinterest strategy.
- It allows you to run a wide range of Pinterest ads.
- It also allows you to set up a shop.

Follow these steps to set up an account:

Step 1: Create a new account

- Go to pinterest.com and click "Sign up."
- Scroll to the bottom of the pop-up and click "Get started here!"
- Fill in your brand's details, including a professional email, your age, and a secure password. Ensure that the email you provided is not connected to another Pinterest account.
- After that, click "Create account."

Step 2: Fill in your business profile details

The site will prompt you to build your business profile. You will provide details such as name, language, and location, then click "Next."

After that, provide a description of your business. The description should include what your business does and include a link to your website. You are now ready to start Pinning and running adverts.

Suppose you have a personal account; you can switch it to a business account. Here is how to do it:

- Log into your Personal account on Pinterest and navigate to the "Settings" tab.
- Select account settings and scroll down to "Account Changes."
- Click "Convert account" under the "Convert to a business account" section.
- After that, fill out your business information such as name, language, location, and description.

Another option would be to link your Pinterest business account to your already-existing personal account. You can do this by:

- Clicking "Add an account" from the settings tab while you are logged into your personal account.
- Under the "Create a free business account," click "Create."
- After that, follow the same steps as mentioned before.

Important Pinterest Terms you should know:

- **Pinner:** a pinner is a person who uses Pinterest.
- **Pins:** Pins are the basic posts published on Pinterest, such as images or videos.
- **Promoted Pins:** These are some kind of Pinterest ads that brands pay to enable more Pinners to see them.
- **Repins:** This is similar to a Facebook share or a Twitter retweet. It is when someone Pins a post they like to one of their boards.
- **Rich Pins:** These Pins automatically pull more details from your brand's website to the Pin. They are used to provide more information like up-to-date pricing. Rich Pins can be in the form of Article Rich Pins, Recipe Rich Pins, and Product Rich Pins.
- **Video Pins:** These are Pins that feature a video that loops.
- **Carousel Pins:** These pins feature up to five images.
- **Collections Pins:** This Pin allows Pinners to shop for similar products.
- **Idea Pins:** You can use these Pins to promote your brand by tailoring the colors and fonts of your Pin, curating collections, or creating a step-by-step guide.
- **Boards:** Think of Pinterest boards as digital mood boards. You can use boards to save, collect and organize your Pins. A great way would be to group the Pins into topics or themes.
- **Group boards:** They are similar to standard boards, but more than one person can add content.
- **Secret Boards:** Only the board's creators and invited collaborators can see this board.

PINTEREST ALGORITHM

The Pinterest algorithm determines the Pins that appear on a user's feed and search results. It continually changes, meaning you must stay up to speed with the latest developments. To ensure the algorithm sees your Pins:

- Use top-quality photos to ensure your Pins are visually appealing.
- Use keywords in your Pin descriptions to ensure your Pins appear in search results.

- Be active on the platform and interact with other users.

Being more active increases your chances of showing up on other users' feeds. The latest development of the algorithm is designed to show users Pins relevant to them based on their past Pins and searches.

How the Pinterest Algorithm works

The Pinterest search algorithm uses several factors to determine the relevance of Pins. The four main factors it considers are:

Domain quality

This refers to the quality of your site. The algorithm detects the popularity of the Pin that came from your site. If the Pin is popular, Pinterest will regard your website as a source of high quality. You can improve your domain quality:

- Ensure your account is a Pinterest Business account to receive website visits, in-depth analytics, and repins.
- Claim a website to show Pinterest that you are an engaged pinner, and that your website source is verified.
- Allow rich pins on your blog. Rich pins contain extra information transferred from your site to the Pin.

Pin quality

The algorithm determines your Pin's quality based on the Pin's popularity and engagement levels. More engagement (likes, comments, and saves) helps your Pin to rank higher. You can improve your Pin quality by:

- Use compelling titles
- Use top-quality images
- Use the correct image sizes

Pinner quality

This refers to the effectiveness of the Pins. This determines how often you Pin, how much interaction the Pins get, and how much you interact with your audience. You can improve pinner quality by:

- Pin popular content
- Pin consistently
- Engage other users more

Topic relevance

Topic relevance will determine whether Pinterest shows your content to other users in their searches. Here is how you can make your topics relevant:

- Perform keyword searches
- Optimize your profile
- Use trending keywords in your Pinterest Pins, boards, and board descriptions

HOW TO USE PINTEREST FOR BUSINESS

Create a Pinterest marketing strategy

Like other social media marketing platforms, you need a solid marketing strategy. An effective strategy should:

- Have SMART goals.
- Learn about the general audience on Pinterest and the demographics highly likely to use the channel.
- Learn about the specific audience on Pinterest your brand is targeting.
- Look at what your competitors are doing on the platform.
- Plan and incorporate on-brand content for Pinterest.

After creating your strategy, you are ready to start working on your goals.

Pin appealing, captivating content

Pinterest is a visual platform. Therefore, you must produce high-quality, engaging visual content to use it effectively for business. Here are some tips for creating an enchanting Pin:

- **Vertical imagery:** Reports suggest that over 80% of Pinterest users access it on mobile (Hirose, 2022). So shoot for a 2:3 aspect ratio so your images are not cropped awkwardly.

- **Use top-quality image and video quality:** use images and videos that consider Pinterest recommendations to avoid pixelation.
- **Be descriptive:** excellent descriptions help brands enhance SEO, add context to your photos and persuade users to click on links.
- **Text overlay:** It is advisable to include a headline to reinforce your visual message.
- **Attractive branding:** Incorporate your logo in your Pins, so your brand does not get lost in the Repin mix-up. This depends on your brand and Pinterest marketing strategy.
- **Ensure your links are working:** Broken links are not helpful for your brand. Therefore, please ensure that the link to your Pin does not go to a 404. Furthermore, ensure it loads fast to give Pinners a better experience.
- **Be consistent:** Pin consistently. For instance, daily pinning is more effective as it enables your brand to reach a broader audience.

Use different Pin formats

While Pinterest is essentially an image-sharing platform, it is not just about photos. Therefore, ensure you mix it up. For example, you can Pin a video persuading Pinners to shop at your e-store. You can also add multiple photos to a Pin by creating a carousel. This approach will allow you to showcase various products and services in a single Pin.

Additionally, you should remember that not all Pinners come to the platform to look for new brands. Pinners evidently visit the platform for inspiration. For instance, over 80% of Pinners revealed they came to Pinterest to start a new project (Olafson, 2021). Consider including how-to Pins and inspirational boards to offer your audience helpful and exciting content.

Plan your boards carefully

The majority of Pinterest searches are unbranded. In this regard, you can use your brand's boards to reach new Pinners looking for specific topics or interested in learning certain things. An excellent example would be skillfully mixing helpful, engaging, and inspirational content boards with more promotional boards.

Optimize your Pins for SEO

Pinterest is a search engine. Therefore, ensure your brand's Pins can be easily found in a search. For example, include keywords in the description of your Pins, in hashtags, and on boards. Consider using Rich Pins designed to pin new content from your business's website. It also helps avoid duplication of content but boosts your business' Pinterest SEO.

Use different Pinterest ads

Pinterest ads are an excellent way to market your business. Pinterest allows advertisers to target their ads around keywords, location, age, interests, and other metrics and parameters. Consider using detailed audience targeting to reach specific Pinterest users. Examples of detailed audience targeting include:

- People who have interacted with your Pins.
- People who have visited your website.
- People who have interacted with similar content on Pinterest.
- A customized list of subscribers to your newsletter.

Promote your Pinterest profile

This will help to ensure that your loyal followers on other social media platforms know about your Pinterest page. Here is how you can promote your Pinterest profile:

- Provide a link to your Pinterest profile on your business website.
- Include the link in your business email signature.
- Cross promote your Pinterest profile on your brand's other social channels.
- Share the news of your Pinterest profile in your business newsletter.

YOUTUBE MARKETING

Literally everyone watches YouTube. Studies show that more than 75% of Americans aged 15 or older are on YouTube (McLachlan, 2022). On a global scale, YouTube has over 2 billion active users monthly. These numbers make

YouTube the second most popular website globally after Google (Martin, 2021).

YouTube's massive potential makes it an excellent resource for marketing your business. Crowing about your brand and products might not be an effective strategy. Instead, you need a strategy that will help you succeed.

Before we look at how to use YouTube for digital marketing, let's define YouTube Marketing. In simple terms, *YouTube marketing* promotes your brand, product, or service on YouTube. Most brands use integrated tactics that include:

- Harnessing the power of influencers
- Creating organic promotional videos
- Advertising on YouTube

Regardless of your strategy, please ensure you produce the content your target audience wants. You might be thinking that is straightforward, right? Well, it is only simple if you understand what your clients really want and not what you believe they want. This is a trap that many brands fall into. In addition, you must ensure the right people find your videos. Fortunately, YouTube is a search engine, so you can optimize your content for the YouTube Algorithm to reach the right people. Keep reading to find out how you can use YouTube for your business.

CREATE A YOUTUBE CHANNEL

The first step in your YouTube marketing journey is creating a YouTube channel. Because YouTube is part of Google, you must have a Google account to sign up for a YouTube channel. It is advisable to create a new Google account for managing your business.

Here are the simple steps:

1. Create a new Google account.
2. Use your Google account to create a YouTube account.
3. Log into YouTube and create a Brand Account and channel.

Using a Brand Account to manage your YouTube channel is the best approach. For example, a Brand Account allows more than one person in your company to manage and update the channel. In addition, you can keep your personal email private. Above all, it allows you to expand your business later by adding other YouTube channels.

To create your YouTube account, navigate to the YouTube page and click "create a channel" before entering your brand name for the Brand Account. You should also take some time to customize your YouTube channel.

From your channel's dashboard, click "Customize channel," then go through the three tabs: Layout, Branding, and Basic Info. These tabs will help you provide information that will optimize your channel and make it easy for your audience to discover.

In this regard, it will help to use descriptive keywords when filling out this information to help your channel appear in searches. Keyword ideas include your channel's topics, products, industry, and questions your content can answer.

Take advantage of the "Branding" section to upload your brand's art and icons to give your channel a unique look. Note that all your uploads should align with the overall brand and visually connect your YouTube account with other social media platforms and web presence. After that, you'll be ready to upload your first video. However, let's skip that for now and ensure your channel is discoverable.

Is your channel discoverable?

There is no point in having amazing YouTube content that nobody sees, right? Therefore, you need to optimize your content and channel for discovery. Here are the most important tips:

- **Optimize your video titles:** give your videos precise, descriptive, and Google-friendly keywords. Titles are what your users will see first and help the search engine understand what your content is about. Please ensure all your titles are intriguing and punchy and include keywords.
- **Optimize your YouTube channel description:** your description should be precise, clear, and descriptive. Ensure you font-load your

keywords and include links to other playlists. Another excellent idea is to use a table of contents having timestamps to make it effortless for viewers to find what they are looking for.

- **Use tags in moderation:** Filling this section with sensationalist tags is very tempting. However, ensure you only include tags relevant to your content. It also helps to be honest and focus on quality rather than quantity. Tags also enable the YouTube algorithm to understand what your videos are about.
- **Cross-promote:** use your other social media platforms to promote your YouTube channel. You can also include a link to your channel on your website and email signature.

Set Permissions for your YouTube Brand Account

Before you implement your YouTube marketing strategy, you must decide who on your team can access the account. Here are the three options you can use to grant access to your account:

- **Owner:** owners have full rights to edit all company Google properties. An owner can add and remove managers, respond to views, edit business information, and more.
- **Manager:** managers have similar editing powers as owners. However, they cannot add or remove page roles or listings.
- **Communications Manager:** Communication managers respond to reviews and perform other actions. However, they cannot access YouTube's video manager, view analytics, or upload content.

THE YOUTUBE ALGORITHM

The YouTube Algorithm selects videos for viewers inspired by two goals:

1. Finding the right video for every user
2. Persuading them to keep watching.

The algorithm uses three distinct discovery systems, i.e.:

- One that selects videos for the YouTube homepage;

- One that ranks search results; and
- One that chooses suggested videos for viewers to watch next.

According to YouTube, homepage and suggested videos are the leading traffic sources for many channels. Instructional videos, which usually get the most traffic, are an exception.

How the algorithm works

As a brand using YouTube for marketing, you should know the signals the platform uses to decide which videos it shows to people. First, every traffic source is unique. However, what ultimately affects your video's view count is a blend of:

- **Personalization** – the viewer's preferences and history;
- **Performance** – the video's success; and
- **External factors** such as the overall market or audience.

How does YouTube determine its homepage algorithm?

Every time a person visits the YouTube website or app, the algorithm provides various videos it thinks that person would want to watch. This selection is broad because the algorithm has not determined what the viewer wants. It uses these two signals to select videos for the homepage:

- **Performance:** YouTube uses parameters such as click-through rate, likes, dislikes, average view duration, viewer surveys, and average percentage views to measure a video's performance. Therefore, when you upload a video, YouTube shows it to a few viewers on the homepage and offers it to more viewers based on its performance.
- **Personalization:** YouTube is not a trending tab. This will offer your video to someone it thinks is relevant to their interest based on history.

How the suggested video algorithm works

YouTube uses different considerations to suggest which videos you should watch next. The algorithm gets a better idea of what videos a person might want to watch after monitoring their behavior for some time.

Therefore, apart from personalization and performance, the algorithm will recommend videos that are usually watched together, topically related videos, and videos that the user watched in the past. Experts advise you to watch YouTube Analytics to check what other videos your audience watched to get suggestions on topics that interest your audience. Additionally, make a sequel to your most successful video.

How YouTube determines its search algorithm

As mentioned before, YouTube is a search engine, meaning SEO is critical. While someone might go to YouTube searching for a specific video, the algorithm decides how it will rank the search results when you type a search keyword. To get your video ranking near the top, use these tips:

- **Keywords:** the YouTube search algorithm uses keywords in your video's metadata to determine what your video is about. Therefore include the keywords that you want your video to show up when people search.
- **Performance:** Once the algorithm determines what your video is about. It will show it to a few people to test its hypothesis. It will then use the performance parameters mentioned above to determine whether your video appeals to the people looking for your keywords.

Now that your YouTube is ready, it is time to create and upload videos. So, what are the different types of videos you can create for your YouTube Brand Channel?

TYPES OF YOUTUBE VIDEOS

- **Customer Testimonials:** These are short-form interviews with satisfied customers. Such videos will help build your brand's and product's credibility.
- **Explainer and tutorial videos:** These are comprehensive videos that explain how to use a product or several parts of a product or a service. You can also use tutorials to answer customer support questions or explain one of your new product's features.

- **Product demonstration videos:** These are usually on-demand. Here, you create short videos demonstrating the proper use of a product and its benefits.
- **Interviews with thought leaders:** You can also create interviews with industry experts and thought leaders to boost your company's credibility in the sector.
- **YouTube Live:** This allows brands to broadcast live content to their viewers. They are excellent for sharing unfiltered moments allowing your audience to participate by giving their reactions and comments.
- **YouTube Shorts:** YouTube Shorts are vertical, short-form videos you can create or watch on YouTube. You can enhance your Shorts using features such as app-based recording, video segmenting, and musical overlays. These short videos will not disappear unless you delete them. These videos enable brands that cannot reach Gen-Z on TikTok to connect with them using professional-looking, industry-related content using Shorts.
- **Project reviews and case studies:** Use these videos to recap a successful campaign or project. Please include statistics and results.
- **Event videos:** Use such videos to feature in-person experiences at an expo or conference. It is an excellent way to show a crowd's excitement.
- **Video blogs:** You can create daily or weekly video blogs documenting events. Additionally, you can record a video to summarize or highlight a blog post to offer your audience multiple ways of digesting content.

Regardless of the video you create, you need a video script. Here are some tips for writing your video script:

- **Define your goal:** establish what you want to accomplish with your video before you start creating it. For instance, do you want to boost brand awareness? Increase social shares? Or drive inbound website traffic? Ensure you have a singular goal at the beginning of the production process, but it is also okay to have multiple goals.
- **Create a storyboard and write the lines:** a storyboard will provide the blueprint and an outline for your video. An effective storyboard should include:

○ Frame for all significant scenes and location changes

○ Basic descriptive details of scenes

○ Each scene's lines

○ The direction of the camera for motion and shot details.

- **Determine extra multimedia elements:** if your video includes title slides, graphics, or other multimedia elements, plan the placement and content for these pieces in advance. You can incorporate these elements into your storyboards to allow the video content to flow seamlessly.
- **Decide the video's length:** you need to determine the length of your video as you make your storyboard. Note that, on YouTube, videos under two minutes usually have the highest chance of being watched to the end. Therefore, ensure your video is just long enough to deliver critical points. If you are creating a longer video, vary your presentation to keep the viewers engaged.
- **Select a filming location:** in the film industry, this step is called location scouting. Your storyboard will guide you in selecting the location. Find out if you'll need permission to use a particular location. Also, ensure you visit each location before you shoot.

With the prep work done, you are now ready to start shooting your videos. Once your video is ready to upload, YouTube allows you to choose the video thumbnail that will appear in search results, your channel, and on the right-hand column. Upload your own thumbnail.

Besides that, consider adding a watermark to all your videos. The watermark usually serves as a custom subscribe button, which viewers can click anytime when watching the videos.

PROMOTING YOUR YOUTUBE CHANNEL

Once you upload your videos, you need to market your YouTube channel and videos. It might be challenging to rank highly in search results when starting out, so you might need to use other strategies to promote your channel. Here are a few strategies you can use to market your YouTube channel:

- **Social media:** Sharing your YouTube video on other social media platforms is an excellent strategy. However, don't just share the video on your timeline or feed; include relevant #hashtags appropriately to ensure there is a conversation around the video.
- **Blog posts and websites:** You can also market your channels and videos on your blog and website. For example, include a follow icon on your website and blog for your audience to find the channel quickly. You can also create videos to accompany specific blog posts.
- **Email:** Share your new video with users on your email list. Encourage your contacts to watch your videos.
- **Collaborate with others:** If your brand has relationships with other companies, you can collaborate with them to give your channel exposure to a different audience. You can create a video together or any other appropriate partnership strategy.

TIKTOK MARKETING

Businesses can no longer underestimate the power of TikTok. While the app is a procrastination tool for teens, it has severely impacted the modern world's sound and culture. As a result, all savvy businesses worldwide are looking at how they can tap into the power of TikTok marketing. Most of the biggest brand moments on TikTok are hardly planned. If you are not one of the lucky brands that accidentally stumble on TikTok, don't fret, it is still possible to build a successful presence on the platform.

IS TIKTOK MARKETING A "THING?"

Well, TikTok marketing uses TikTok to promote your brand, product, or service. You employ strategies such as influencer marketing, organic viral content, or TikTok advertising. Many brands use TikTok marketing to achieve the following:

- Boost brand awareness
- Build engaged communities
- Offer customer service
- Sell products and services
- Get feedback

- Advertise products and services

There are three main types of TikTok marketing:

Creating your own TikToks

This is an excellent approach as it gives you a lot of freedom. You will need to create a TikTok account to use this approach. You can create videos showing your products, services, or other relevant organic content.

TikTok Influencer marketing

This is part of TikTok's ecosystem. Megastars on the platform significantly impact a brand's success because millions of users watch their content daily. However, you don't need a high-profile influencer to market successfully. You can also use rising stars or influencers in your niche.

TikTok Advertising

TikTok is an excellent place to advertise your brand, products, or services. The cost of advertising on the platform is based on a bidding model.

HOW TO SET UP TIKTOK FOR YOUR BUSINESS

TikTok established a TikTok for Business hub in 2020 before launching TikTok Pro a few months later. At first, the two were different, but later TikTok merged them because they provided similar insights. Currently, TikTok for Business is what you need for your brand. You need to create a business account, add more information to your profile, and access real-time insights and metrics. Follow these steps to open a TikTok business account:

1. Visit your profile page.
2. Click on the "Settings and Privacy" tab in the top right corner.
3. Click "Manage account."
4. Under "Account control," select "Switch to Business Account."
5. Select the appropriate category for your business. You can select from: Art & Crafts, Machinery & Equipment, and Personal Blog.
6. After that, add a business website and email to your profile, and you'll be good to go!

Videos are the main content format on TikTok. You can create short videos, but this does not mean you transfer your 30-second TV ad to TikTok, it should be TikTok.

THE TIKTOK ALGORITHM

Before developing your TikTok marketing strategy, it is important to understand how the TikTok algorithm works. The TikTok algorithm comprises several factors with a straightforward goal: to show users content they are most interested in based on their previous engagement. The factors that the algorithm considers include:

- The content you like, share, complete, re-watch, and comment on
- Hashtags and captions you interact with
- The subject matter of your search
- Your account settings such as language preferences, posting location, and device type
- Trending audio in the videos
- The content you have marked as "not interested."

In this sense, it is critical that you get your video content on the "For You" page, which is TikTok's main discovery page. This is an excellent strategy for playing into the app's algorithm. Every content creator on the platform aims to get the TikTok algorithm to place their content on the "For You" page because it puts your content before as many viewers as possible.

Here is how you can play into the algorithm:

Give user-generated content priority

User-generated content comes in different forms. It is content actual TikTok users have created. When you prioritize UGC, it enables you to build audience loyalty. This is because over 50% of TikTok users feel closer to brands that publish unpolished content that features "normal" people.

UGC is also famous because viewers find it more authentic. After all, it is created by actual customers that love your brand. Users can also highlight your product's or service's value without being compensated. Moreover, consumers willingly support a brand they trust, and authenticity is something Gen-Zers value.

Encourage users to tag you in their social media posts to enable you to generate UGC. Also, save content from users that you can repost on your brand's profile. Finally, as you repost UGC, make sure you give credit to the original creator. You can use these two features to repost:

- **Duets:** This allows you to repost by cutting the screen in half so your repost and the original play side by side.
- **Stitch:** This feature allows you to take other video parts and use them in your content.

Build a good relationship with influencers

Influencers are very popular on TikTok. In fact, nearly 25% of all the content on the platform features an influencer or celebrity. These content creators usually generate massive buzz for your brand when they share your products with their audiences. Therefore, influencers will help expand your reach, giving you an algorithmic boost by putting your products and services before more eyes.

However, if you are a small business, you might not have the resources to get the services of influencers. Consider using micro-influencers who have a more dedicated following and high engagement. Their services are relatively lower than major influencers.

You can manually research your own influencers by checking your competitor pages and mining the comments for highly engaged users who have their own following. These are great candidates to use as micro-influencers.

TikTok ads should be your priority

Advertising on TikTok will transform how you view digital marketing. According to studies, UGC-based ads on TikTok usually outperform other digital placements, including Facebook ads and other digital ads (Kalehoff, 2022). These numbers are convincing enough to have you rethink your social media marketing budget. Consider decreasing your budget spend on other digital ad placements in favor of TikTok.

Study trending audio

Music and sound have a significant impact on engagement with TikTok. As a result, they boost the chances of your content being viewed. According to a study by TikTok (TikTok, 2022):

- 67% of users would like to view TikTok videos from brands that feature trending audio.
- 68% of TikTok users claim that trending audio enables them to remember the brand effortlessly.
- 58% of TikTokers stated they are highly likely to share an ad that has trending sounds.
- 62% said they are eager to learn about a brand after watching a video featuring trending sounds.

In this regard, it is critical to include trending audio in your videos. However, TikTok trends change daily, so how will you know the trendiest sounds?

Click "Discover" at the bottom of your screen, and you will see a scrolling feed featuring all the trending hashtags and sounds on TikTok. Keep scrolling until you see an icon in a circle on the left of a music note. On the right side, you will see a number that shows how many videos on the app feature the sound.

TikTok also allows you to snag a sound directly from another TikToker's video as long as it is licensed for TikTok. Tap the spinning, circular icon at the bottom right of the screen to get a piece of audio from a video. TikTok will show you all the videos with that sound using a red button at the bottom center labeled "Use this sound."

Track engagement using analytics

Your TikTok Business account lets you keep track of your account's analytics to discover the things your target audience loves and use the information to refine your content. The advantage of monitoring your posts' performance is that it eliminates guesswork from your TikTok marketing strategy.

The in-app analytics are divided into four categories:

- **Overview** – keeps track of engagement and followers.
- **Content** – tracks your favorite videos.
- **Followers** – analyzes audience growth and demographics.
- **Live**: shows insights from your live videos.

TIKTOK MARKETING STRATEGY

TikTok trends look random, but as a marketer, you know that a surefire marketing strategy is a fallacy. Therefore, you need elaborate steps to help your business perform well on the app. Use this blueprint to create a TikTok marketing strategy:

Familiarize yourself with TikTok

You cannot approach TikTok marketing the way you would on other social media platforms. TikTok is very different, having unique features, trends, and user behaviors. Spend some time watching TikTok videos and exploring various features on the app, such as filters, effects, and trending songs.

Examine how branded hashtag challenges that involve dance moves, songs, or tasks members are challenged to recreate. Ensure you find out how the TikTok algorithm works.

Identify your target audience

Who do you want to reach on the app? TikTok is popular among the younger generation. You should also take some time to research your audience on other social media platforms to look for the overlap on TikTok. Also, be open to reaching a new audience.

While your current audience might be on TikTok, there could be other subgroups with related to or slightly different interests on the platform. Once you decide on the target audience, find out the types of content they love and interact with.

Analyze your competition

If your competitors are on TikTok, check out what the top three similar brands are doing on the platform. Find out what has worked and has backfired. It would also help to seek the assistance of influencers and other personalities. They can help you come up with a great strategy.

Set goals that are in line with your business objectives

While you can create TikToks for fun, have goals tied to your overall business objectives. As mentioned in Chapter 1, your goals should be SMART.

Post regularly

Create a content calendar and stick to it. Your TikTok calendar will help you know when to "Go Live" or when to upload a "New Video." Luckily, there are multiple tools you can use to implement this strategy.

Track progress

Every strategy must have a mechanism for tracking progress. This will help you gauge whether your approach is effective. Check regularly how you are performing compared to your goals.

Create room for experimentation

No single formula can help your brand go viral on TikTok. You can follow strategies that work for other brands but ensure you leave space in your plan to have fun, be creative and go with the flow. If something backfires, pick your lessons and move on to the next experiment.

LINKEDIN MARKETING

Linked Marketing uses LinkedIn to generate leads, make connections, foster business relationships and partnerships, and improve brand awareness. LinkedIn is integral to many successful marketing strategies because of its expanding professional networks.

You can use LinkedIn to drive traffic to your website, share your expertise using thought-leadership content and identify quality leads. It is also an excellent platform for marketing job openings and attracting fresh talent to your team.

HOW TO CREATE A LINKEDIN ACCOUNT FOR YOUR BRAND

Step 1: Add your business

You must have a LinkedIn personal account to do this. Click the "Work" icon on the top left of your LinkedIn page and then click "Create Company Page." The platform will allow you to select the type of company you are creating the page for small business, medium to large business, showcase page, or educational institution.

After that, provide your company's official name and add a URL to enable your audience to find your business quickly. Add your brand's website URL to offer your audience direct access to the site.

Step 2: Enter company details

Provide company details, including industry, size, and type. Select the best description from the drop-down menu.

Step 3: Add a logo and create a company description

Upload your company logo to act as your LinkedIn profile picture. After that, add a brief, snappy tagline that tells your audience about your brand. LinkedIn will display this at the top of your page next to your company logo. Check the box indicating that you are acting on behalf of your company, then click "Create Page."

Step 4: Create a company description

Use this section to tell your audience more about your business. You have 2000 characters to do this. Note that the first 156 characters are critical because they will appear in your page's Google preview. Include up to 20 company specialties using keywords to help people find your business on LinkedIn.

Step 5: Publish the page

If you are happy with the description and the tags you've chosen, click "Publish," and your LinkedIn page will go live.

HOW TO INCORPORATE LINKEDIN INTO YOUR SOCIAL MEDIA CONTENT STRATEGY

Use hashtags

You can use hashtags to add emphasis to your LinkedIn post. You can also use them to tap into new niches, audiences, and industries. Find the right balance between relevant and popular hashtags because using too many or the wrong ones can hinder your reach.

Query a broad hashtag from the search bar. For example, if you are in the growth market, you can start by searching #growthmarketing to see the number of people following the hashtag and how often it is used.

After that, start with around five hashtags to reach your target audience. Consider using hashtags with varying followings. For example, you can use lesser-known hashtags to narrow your reach to an audience likely to engage your content on LinkedIn.

LinkedIn Profile vs. LinkedIn Page

People can follow a LinkedIn Page without sending a connection request and waiting for approval. Therefore, when other users share your page with their connections, they can follow it. Profiles are private and are mainly used by individuals. You can also have private conversations with connections that join your network.

The two entities can work together to create the ultimate marketing work-flow. For instance, you can include yourself as an employee of your business and list your brand's LinkedIn Page as your employer in your personal profile. This way, when someone lands on your profile, they can also see your Page.

Create posts with varying lengths

You can create both short and long-form stories on your LinkedIn Page. Long posts usually capture the reader's attention causing them to dwell longer on the app. However, don't be the person that shares mono-logues because your network might not always have the time to read them. Sharing too many short posts might come across as lacking substance, making you lose your position as a thought leader. Therefore, vary the length of your content to keep it fresh and relevant to your network.

Share external content on the platform

The LinkedIn algorithm supports external links to websites and blogs. However, the content must be relevant to your audience. It is not a must to credit the author, but using their hashtag to give them credit might encourage them to share your post with their followers. Also, if they comment on your post, it will introduce your profile to their audience.

Have a consistent publishing schedule

LinkedIn is known as the platform with the most extended lifespans. There-fore, it does not require you to have a round-the-clock publishing schedule. However, it needs to be consistent. Posting regularly enables you to build trust. Choose a realistic schedule and stick to it.

HOW TO USE LINKEDIN FOR BUSINESS AND MARKETING

Use a custom public Profile URL

Customize your LinkedIn public profile to make it look more professional and easier to share. To do this, click "View Profile" then "Edit Public Profile and URL." Change your URL to anything you like, like your business name, as long as another user has not taken it.

Add a background photo to your profile

Add an on-brand background photo to give your LinkedIn Profile more personality. LinkedIn provides one for you, but you can update it to display your special interests and personal brand. Stick to size recommendations.

Edit your Profile

Consider editing and reordering sections of your LinkedIn Profile. This will enable you to highlight specific information.

Optimize your profile for search engines

You can optimize your profile to be discovered by others by searching LinkedIn for the keywords you want to be found for. Please add relevant keywords to different sections of your profile, such as headline, summary, and work experience.

Add a ProFinder Badge to your Profile

The ProFinder Badge is used to identify freelancers within LinkedIn's ProFinder. This is a service that matches contractors to project managers seeking help. You can display the badge on your profile to show prospective clients your skills, expertise, and experience.

Harness the power of blog and website links on your LinkedIn Profile

Consider adding portfolio links and social networks to your LinkedIn page. You can also add links to your content and business information to increase clicks. This approach enables you to draw greater attention to specific areas of your page and drive traffic elsewhere.

Check your Network updates

Network Updates is LinkedIn's version of Facebook News Feed. Check out this feed to find out what your connections, competitors, customers, and others are sharing. You can also share your own updates, such as product details or services or any other relevant content your brand has created.

Be identifiable

It should be effortless for your connections to identify your profile when they see it. Therefore, ensure your name, headline, and other identifiers are visible. Also, enable the Public Profile settings to make it visible and identifiable to your target audience.

Join LinkedIn Groups

LinkedIn Groups enable you to connect with people working or interested in your industry. They are also a hub where you can share content, boost brand awareness, grow your contact list and establish yourself as an expert in your industry. Furthermore, participating in group discussions can inspire thought leadership in your industry.

You can also create your own group to cement your position as a thought leader in your sector. The group will also help you grow a community of advocates, generate new leads, generate new marketing content ideas, and promote brand awareness.

LINKEDIN MARKETING OPTIONS

There are four main ad types of ads you can use on LinkedIn. Each is designed to achieve different brand goals. They include:

- **Sponsored Content:** LinkedIn's homepage for users has a newsfeed custom to each profile's network. Sponsored content shows up on feeds and reaches a highly engaged audience. This content is usually labeled as "promoted" and stands out from the regular newsfeed.
- **Sponsored messages:** LinkedIn users have an inbox to connect with other users. Very few businesses use messaging to interact with potential leads. Therefore, it is an excellent opportunity to get ahead of the competition.
- **Lead Gen Forms:** Collecting user information streamlines the process of converting leads. Lead gen forms are pre-filled forms that enable you to collect and record leads on LinkedIn.
- **Text Ads:** LinkedIn has a right rail that can feature ads. These ads can be text, spotlight, or followers and are more condensed than sponsored content.

LINKEDIN ALGORITHM

LinkedIn might seem all business, but it is a social network. Like other social networks, it depends on an algorithm to send content to its users. Knowing how to appease the algorithm can work in your favor.

How it works

Check whether your post is spam or genuine content

The algorithm uses several factors to check whether the content is relevant to the audience. It does this by sorting content into the following categories:

- **Spam:** The algorithm flags your content as spam if it uses poor grammar or includes multiple links. Therefore, avoid posting too frequently and tagging too many people.
- **Low-quality**: This is not spam but it does not follow content best practices. If your post is not engaging, the algorithm considers it low-quality.
- **High-quality**: These are posts that adhere to LinkedIn content recommendations such as:

  - easy to read

  - uses three or fewer hashtags

  - encourages responses

  - includes strong keywords

  - tags people who are likely to respond

It tests your post

Once the algorithm establishes that your content is genuine, it pushes it to a few of your followers. It will push it to more people if it attracts lots of engagement. However, if no one is interested or worse, someone flags your post as spam or hides it from their feed, LinkedIn will not bother sharing it. Here are tips to pass this test:

- post at the time you know your followers are online
- user questions to spark engagement
- respond to questions and comments
- post consistently
- interact with other posts

It delivers your content to more people

If your post attracts a lot of engagement, the algorithm will send your content to a broader audience. It will primarily target people you are closely connected to, those interested in the topic, and those likely to engage with the content.

TWITTER MARKETING

Twitter is a powerful social networking tool and search engine that attracts people from all walks of life. You can find the latest information on virtually any topic, including updates from businesses and companies. Your business can market on Twitter, engage users and followers, boost brand awareness, and increase conversions. The platform also makes it effortless to distribute content to over 326 million users who use it monthly.

It would help if you had a Twitter marketing strategy to use the platform effectively. Your strategy will help you create a plan for creating, publishing, and distributing your content to your audience, followers, and buyer personas. Your strategy should attract new leads and followers, improve brand recognition, and boost conversions and sales.

Twitter is a unique marketing tool because:

- It is free to use
- It expands your brand's reach
- Allows brands to share and promote branded content
- Will enable brands to offer quick customer care support
- Prospects use it as a search engine tool to find and learn about your brand
- Brands can use it as a search engine tool to search for their competitors and their marketing content

HOW TO USE TWITTER FOR YOUR BRAND

Customize and brand your profile

When someone visits your company's Twitter profile, they should automatically know it is yours. Therefore, customize and brand your Twitter account with your logo, brand colors, and any other recognizable details you want to include. Here's how to customize your profile:

- **Handle:** This is your username and should include your company's name to make it effortless for your prospects to find.

- **Header:** This refers to the background image. Use something unique to your brand, like your logo or other branded image.
- **Profile picture:** Your profile picture on Twitter represents your brand's interaction, posts, and tweets on the platform. Use something that clearly defines your company, such as your logo or company initials.
- **Bio:** Here, provide a synopsis of your business in 160 characters. You can include your mission statement. Make it engaging and humorous.
- **Website URL:** Include your brand website's URL to direct traffic to your website.
- **Birthday:** Use this information to inform your audience about your company's establishment.

Create Twitter lists

This is an organized group of Twitter accounts you select and put in specific categories. When you open a Twitter List, you will only see tweets by users on the list. Twitter lists are great if you want to follow specific accounts. You can use groups to segment your list, including competitors, business inspiration, and target audience. This makes it effortless for you to review their content, posts, and interactions.

Host a Twitter Chat

Brands host Twitter chats to engage their followers, create a sense of community, discuss a topic and get the opinion of their audience. To host a Twitter chat (TweetChat), choose a topic, set the time and date, and create a hashtag for the TweetChat. Share this information with your audience using a Tweet on your website or Twitter bio.

Everyone who wants to participate in the chat can see all responses, questions, and comments on the topic of discussion. They can also share their comments and thoughts by using the hashtag in their comments. TweetChats promote interaction and engagement with your profile and boost your brand awareness. They also enable brands to establish a more personal experience with their audiences.

Advertise on Twitter

Twitter adverts are an excellent way of reaching your audience. They enable your tweets to reach thousands of Twitter users, increasing your following and influence. You can achieve this through:

Promoted Tweets

Promoted Tweets enable your tweets to appear in Twitter streams or search results of particular users. This is an excellent option for brands looking to get more people on a specific web page. You will have to pay a monthly fee to use this feature.

Twitter puts your promoted tweets in a daily campaign targeting the audience profile you want to reach, as you indicated in the settings. All Twitter users can interact with your Twitter Ads as they would your organic content.

Twitter Ads

This is an excellent option for brands to use different tweets to achieve one goal. They also help brands that want to grow their user base and brand awareness. The objectives you can choose from for your Twitter Ads include website conversions, video views, and app installations. Your decision will impact the price you pay to run the ad.

Drive traffic to your website

Twitter is an excellent tool to use to drive traffic to your website. You can achieve this in several ways, including putting a website URL on your profile and adding links to your blogs, tweets, and web pages.

Twitter Moments

These are a collection of tweets about a specific event or topic. Twitter moments are like the "best of" collection of tweets on a given topic. For instance, Twitter's Moments section includes "Fun," "News," "Today," and "Entertainment." Twitter also allows you to create your own Moments section that your followers can view from your profile.

You can also group your Twitter Moments to enable you to market your brand's events and campaigns. They also play an integral role in your marketing strategy, allowing your brand to promote discussions on specific topics.

Get Verified

Apply to get your brand's Twitter profile verified depending on its size and industry. According to Twitter, you can only apply for verification if you are in music, fashion, acting, government, religion, politics, media, sports, journalism, and other key interest areas. If Twitter accepts your application and verifies your profile, your handle will have a badge with a blue checkmark. This is essential as it confirms that your account is authentic.

Build your follower count

It goes without saying that having more Twitter followers means more people viewing and interacting with your content. Therefore, focus on building your follower count to increase your chances of boosting brand awareness and direct more traffic to your brand's website.

How can you build your follower count?

- Use unique hashtags
- Ensure your content is sharable
- Use Twitter influencers
- Create engaging content like surveys, questions, contests, and giveaways
- Include links to your Twitter profile on your website
- Interact with your followers and retweet their content to encourage them to do the same for you.

TWITTER ALGORITHM

Twitter has several algorithms that determine all aspects of how it serves content on the platform. Many marketers refer to the Twitter algorithm as the one that powers the Home feed timeline. This is also referred to as the top Tweets view.

Twitter describes the Twitter feed algorithm as a stream of Tweets from the accounts you follow, and recommendations of other content the algorithm thinks might interest you. It decides this by looking at the tweets you interact with frequently.

The algorithm does not affect your main timeline if you are using the Latest Tweets view. It only structures the timeline of people using the Home view.

HOW THE ALGORITHM WORKS

Home timeline vs. latest tweets

You can toggle between the Home or Latest Tweets Twitter timelines. Latest Tweets displays tweets from people you follow in a real-time chronological timeline. For the Home timeline, Twitter shuffles posts into what it suggests is a better order.

Customizable timelines

You can use Twitter Lists to create a custom timeline. Twitter allows you to pin up to five lists for easy access. Also, each list will enable you to toggle between Top Tweets and Latest Tweets like in the main timeline. You can also access tweets from the lists you follow on your Home timeline.

Twitter Topics

Twitter uses an algorithm to suggest topics based on what it thinks you like. For example, if you follow a topic, the algorithm will show tweets, events, and ads in your timeline.

Trends

You can find Twitter trends on your Home timeline, notifications, search results, and profile pages. The Twitter trending topic algorithm decides which topics appear as Trends. Sometimes it is evident, while at other times, it is a mystery you must solve! By default, the trending topic algorithm shows trends based on user location.

Recommended accounts

The Twitter algorithm suggests accounts you might like. You can check this on your Home screen, Explore tab, and profile page. It makes these recommendations based on:

- Twitter Activity
- Activity on third-party sites with integrated Twitter content
- Contacts
- Location
- Promoted accounts

Twitter algorithm ranking signals

Twitter states that it ranks top tweets based on the accounts you interact with most. Here are the signals Twitter uses:

- **Recency:** For trends, the Twitter algorithm focuses on topics that are trendy now. Current events and issues usually appear in the "What's Happening" section at the top of the Home timeline.
- **Relevance:** The algorithm checks your previous actions, accounts you've interacted with, and topics you follow and engage with most for relevance. It also checks your location and the number of Tweets related to a particular topic.
- **Engagement:** For tweets, the algorithm checks how popular the tweet is and how people in your network engage it. It also checks how much people are tweeting, retweeting, liking, and replying to topics. Lastly, for trends, the algorithm checks the number of tweets related to the trend.
- **Rich media:** The algorithm looks at the type of media included in the tweet.

Here are some quick tips for working with the Twitter algorithm:

- Be active on Twitter to boost brand visibility and grow engagement.
- Ensure your account is verified to boost your credibility.
- Tweet promptly for better interaction.
- Use hashtags strategically.
- Post different content formats such as photos, videos, and GIFs.
- Encourage your followers to participate in your posts by asking for feedback.
- Take advantage of Twitter Polls to get your followers' views on different topics.

- Participate in relevant trends and topics to boost your odds of appearing on a Twitter Moment.
- Consider repackaging top content to reach followers who might have missed that tweet the first time.
- Use insights from Twitter Analytics to refine your Twitter marketing strategy.

SNAPCHAT MARKETING

Snapchat is an ideal marketing tool for a brand that wants to connect with people under 35. The platform went live in 2011 and has established itself as one of the most used social media platforms globally. While it might not attract as many users as Facebook and YouTube, it is still an effective way to reach a new audience. The platform attracts around 319 million active users, creating Snaps and sending them daily.

Why your business should use Snapchat

First, it is critical to note that Snapchat might not be the ideal social media platform for every business. However, there are compelling reasons why your brand should use Snapchat:

Reach a younger demographic

If your brand wants to connect with people aged 35 and below, Snapchat is a great tool. Data from Snapchat revealed that the platform reaches 75% of Gen Z and Millennials. It also reaches 23% of American adults (Macready, 2022). Evidently, Snapchat is an engaging social media platform for the younger generation.

Encourage users to interact with your brand

Users can discover new businesses as they interact with their friends on Snapchat. The platform's current design connects friends through the "Chat" button. It connects users with brands and content creators through the Discover button.

Therefore, Snapchatters use the Discover icon to view content by brands that use the platform for marketing their products and services.

Stand out and showcase your brand's humorous side

Snapchat was designed to be fun and casual. It is all about being real and not picture-perfect. That's why it calls itself the app for #RealFriends. Most of its features focus on creativity, humor, and being cheeky.

SETTING UP SNAPCHAT FOR YOUR BRAND

You need a Snapchat Business account to use it for marketing effectively. The business account allows you to do more than you would with a standard version. For example, you can access more features to support your marketing strategy.

The business account also allows you to create a Public Profile for your brand. This gives your company a permanent landing page on the platform. Some of the advantages of using a Snapchat Business account are:

- You can advertise on the platform using the Ads Manager.
- You can age-target your content to reach a particular audience.
- You can also perform location-targeting to reach people in a specific area.

Here is how to create your Snapchat Business account:

1. **Download the app:** The Snapchat app is available on App Store and Google Play Store.
2. **Create an account:** If you are not on Snapchat, create your user account first.
3. **Create a Business Account:** With your personal account set up, access the Snapchat Business Manager to create a Business account. Provide your brand's legal name, your name, and choose the country your business will be operating in and select your currency. After that, Snapchat creates your Business account automatically.
4. **Start snapping and creating campaigns:** your Business account is now ready to start advertising campaigns to reach your target audience. Remember, keep your content fun and quirky.

Snapchat Business Manager

Snapchat Business Manager is your brand's one-stop platform for producing, launching, observing, and optimizing your Snapchat account. It offers built-in business management tools like custom ad targeting, product catalogs, and analytics. These features allow brands to generate engaging and exciting content.

The notable Snapchat Business Manager features are:

- **Instant create:** This allows you to create a single image or video ad in a short time.
- **Advanced create:** Use this feature to generate in-depth campaigns. You can streamline your objectives, split test your ads and create new sets.
- **Events manager:** This feature lets you connect your website to a Snap Pixel, which examines the cross-channel effectiveness of your ads.
- **Catalogs:** With this feature, brands can upload product inventories directly to the platform, creating a flawless buying experience.
- **Lens Web Builder Tool:** Brands can use this tool to create custom AR lenses to delight their audiences. It comes with pre-set templates.
- **Create filters:** This feature enables brands to use branded illustrations or images to connect with their audience in Snaps.
- **Audience insights:** This integral functionality allows brands to learn more about their clients.
- **Creator marketplace:** Use this feature to partner with other top Snapchat creators for their campaigns.

HOW TO USE SNAPCHAT FOR BUSINESS

Inform your audience about your Snapchat account

If your Snapchat account is new, let your audience know about it. You can do this by:

- Cross-promote your Snapchat username on other social media platforms like Facebook and Twitter.

- Create a custom Snapcode. This is a badge that people can scan with their phones to find your brand effortlessly. Snapcodes also allow users to find your brand's unique lenses, filters, and content.
- Include the Snapcode or URL to your marketing materials. A Snapcode does not have to be viewed on the screen to work; you can also include it in your marketing merchandise. Snapchat users can use their devices to find you on the platform by scanning your code from a business card or T-shirt.

Create an effective marketing strategy

A good Snapchat marketing strategy must include the following:

- **Objective:** What your brand hopes to achieve on Snapchat and how you will measure success.
- **Have a content calendar:** know when you will post, what you will post and the time you will spend engaging your followers.
- **Choose your brand's tone and look:** ensure your Snapchat presence is consistent with your presence elsewhere.

Know your Snapchat audience and their metrics

Please take advantage of Snapchat Insights to see the people viewing your content and how they are performing. This will help you understand if you are achieving your goals. Some metrics you should consider are:

- **Views:** How many story views does your brand get weekly and monthly? Also, check the time users spend viewing your stories.
- **Reach:** the number of Snapchatters your content reaches daily.
- **Demographic information:** the age, location, and lifestyle of your audience.

Interact with your Snapchat audience

Snapchat separates content from brands from content from friends and family. This split screen design demands that you engage with your audience to maintain your presence. Ideas for engaging with your audience include:

- Follow other Snapchatters
- View Snaps and stories by other users
- View any Snaps sent to you
- Partner with brands and creators
- Respond to Snaps and instant messages others send to you
- Create content regularly

Take advantage of Snapchat's many features to create engaging content

Snaps are designed to disappear. Luckily, you can do a lot to enhance a simple image or video, making it more inviting. The features you should take advantage of are:

- Write captions over Snaps
- Include polling
- Draw over a Snap
- Use several Snaps to share a narrative
- Include background music to Snaps
- Add information like location, time, and temperature
- Add a Snapchat lens
- Add a Snapchat filter

Take advantage of sponsored AR lenses

Snapchat's artificial reality (AR) lenses change how users experience the world. They achieve this by superimposing digital effects, graphics, and animations on real-life images. Furthermore, users can interact with the superimposed image.

Design a sponsored geofilter

Geofilters are simple overlays for a Snap. You can use them from a specific area and for a limited time. For example, you can add an emoji or sticker with details such as location.

Use various ad formats for advertising on Snapchat

For your Snapchat marketing strategy to be effective, consider incorporating different advertising formats such as:

- Snap ads
- Story ads
- Collection ads
- Dynamic ads

Apart from increasing brand awareness, these adverts will also help drive traffic to your website and boost sales. Your ads should target a specific audience.

Stay updated with the latest features

These new features will help you revise your Snapchat content strategy. Here are some features to consider:

- **Snaps in 3D:** This feature gives your Snaps an additional dimension such that when users wiggle their phones, they experience the 3D effect.
- **Custom landmarkers:** This AR lens enables users to build location-based lenses that only work in specific locations. Brands can create custom landmarkers for their stores or anything meaningful for their fans.
- **Bitmoji branded outfits:** This quirky integration allows your Bitmoji to wear clothes from brands recognized globally. Users can also share their favorite Bitmoji outfits with their friends.

Make your business easy to find

Use features such as Swipe Up to Call and Swipe Up to Text for your brand. Moreover, users can swipe up to visit your brand's website.

SNAPCHAT ALGORITHM

Snapchat's algorithm shows users the most engaging Snaps that could interest them. The algorithm's objective is to serve the right snaps, to the right users, at the right time. It also organizes the content based on relevance to the user.

How the algorithm works

Snapchat has different features and functionalities, each with its own algorithm.

They include:

- **Snapchat algorithm for best friends:** Snapchat depends on your contacts. It considers the people you Snap and Chat with most as your best friends. Their profiles appear on the "Send To" screen after you send them a Snap. They will also appear on the Chat section of your profile.
- **Snapchat's discover algorithm:** The Discover algorithm differentiates between personal content and content created by professional media. The Discover feature will help you access stories from media outlets, brands, and influencers.
- **Snapchat algorithm for Quick Add:** This algorithm decides who appears on your Quick Add suggestions list. It uses your contacts, people you are in Group chats with, and mutual friends to determine who to add to the list.
- **Snapchat algorithm for story views:** Snapchat stories usually go in chronological order. However, with this algorithm, the more stories you post, the more people can view them.
- **Snapchat spotlight algorithm:** This algorithm works by understanding your personal preferences to serve Snaps that you might be interested in.
- **Snapchat face detection algorithm:** this is the algorithm that makes Snapchat's filters more realistic and fun. It identifies your unique facial structures and features as Haar Features. It then uses the Active Shape Model to sense all your facial features.

KEY TAKEAWAYS

- There are many social media platforms available. Each works best for different marketing scenarios.
- It is advisable to understand how a social media platform works before you start using it for your brand.

- Analyze what your competition is doing and learn from their successes and failures.
- Your social media goals should align with your overall goals.

CHAPTER 5
EMAIL MARKETING

Email marketing is one of the oldest forms of digital marketing. Still, it remains one of the most effective digital marketing strategies for brands. While there are new communication methods like live chats and social media, email remains the best marketing channel.

Reports suggest that email marketing has an ROI of $36 for every dollar you spend (Litmus, 2022). This means it deserves a place in your marketing toolbox. Moreover, email marketing was ranked higher than other methods such as SEO, social media, and affiliate marketing (Dormer, 2021). So why is email marketing still effective in an era where new channels have taken all the headlines?

Despite the growth of social media, many people still use email more than other marketing platforms. Furthermore, studies have also shown that many people are on email, making it a very effective marketing tool.

Additionally, email marketing allows you to own connections, and you don't have to worry about an algorithm changing the ranking of your reach.

FUNDAMENTALS OF EMAIL MARKETING

Before looking at email marketing strategies, it is essential to look at the fundamentals. They include:

- **Stay human:** Email marketing is very competitive. It helps to use email to speak directly to your prospects. Also, mention their names and allow them to see your human side.
- **Use engaging titles:** Please don't bait and switch. Use intriguing subject titles to persuade users to open your emails. However, ensure you keep them on topic and avoid being spammy. If users feel duped, they can unsubscribe or mark your email as spam, affecting your deliverability.
- **Keep the messages precise:** Most people read emails on their mobile devices. Therefore, keep your copy clear. Suppose you want to share more information and direct users to a landing page or blog post.
- **Use CTAs:** Include CTAs at the top and bottom of your email, probably after the first paragraph and towards the end.
- **Ask permission and fulfill your promises:** Avoid buying email lists. It is illegal and will not deliver ROI. Also, if you offer great content or deals, ensure you provide top-quality content or offers.

TYPES OF EMAIL MARKETING

Remember the sales funnel? People at different stages of the sales funnel need different types of information. You need to consider this factor when creating your emails. Here, we'll look at different email marketing types you can use for different scenarios. The most common email marketing types include:

Welcome Emails

Initial contact with your prospects usually finds them unprepared to do business. According to studies, only 25% of leads are sales-ready immediately, and 50% are qualified but not ready to buy. In this regard, you need to nurture these leads to push them down the sales funnel.

Effective welcome emails should offer a personal touch and introduce your brand without a sales pitch. Build a relationship without introducing a new product or service. Your goal is to give an excellent first impression illustrating your expertise and grasp of the industry.

Email Newsletters

Many brands use email newsletters to remain top of mind for their users. For example, most industrial businesses typically use email newsletters as the foundation of their email marketing strategy because they are excellent for educating customers and prospects about your brand. You can also use the newsletters to display employee profiles, relevant graphics, and company passion projects.

Newsletters also help nurture prospects and existing customers using product announcements, company events, and feedback requests. The ongoing communication also helps to retain happy customers and obtain helpful feedback.

Dedicated Emails

These are also known as standalone emails. They contain information about a single offer. For example, you can inform your audience about a new white paper you have released. You can also use dedicated emails to invite them to an event you are hosting.

A dedicated email can also help you set the stage to introduce the main call-to-action, making them similar to landing pages. You can reach your entire database with dedicated emails.

Lead Nurturing Emails

This is an inbound marketing strategy that involves understanding your leads' needs and timing. In this sense, it is critical to define your buyer personas to enable you to reach your target audience effectively.

Lead nurturing uses a closely connected series of emails that have a logical purpose and are full of helpful content. As a result, these types of emails offer more benefits than an individual blast email.

Furthermore, promotional emails are multifaceted because you can design them to promote multiple things. A few things you can promote include marketing materials like webinars, blog posts, and eBooks. You can also use lead nurturing emails to inform your customers about what is happening in your company.

Ensure you create different promotional nurturing emails to cater to user needs based on their position in the sales funnel. This will ensure you provide helpful content to your prospects.

Sponsorship Emails

Sponsorship emails will help you reach a different audience and get new leads. A sponsorship usually involves paying to include your copy in another vendor's newsletter. They form part of a paid media strategy, including display advertising, pay-per-click (PPC), affiliate advertising, and mobile advertising.

You'll need to create your email copy as per the vendor's specifications. Stick to the partner's size restrictions and image suggestions. Provide both plain text and HTML versions in advance. Please ensure the partner you choose is credible and understands your business needs.

Transactional Emails

These are messages triggered by specific actions taken by your contacts and usually help them complete that action. For example, after you sign up for an industry webinar, you fill out a form and receive a transactional email giving you login information to join. Transactions are also emails you receive from eCommerce sites confirming your order and providing shipping information.

Re-Engagement Emails

Suppose metrics show that some of your subscribers have been inactive; it would help send out a re-engagement email to re-establish goodwill and contact. A great approach would be to ask for feedback; if they respond, you win!

Brand Story Emails

Storytelling is undoubtedly a powerful tool to communicate with prospects and customers by taking advantage of emotional responses. Is there a personal story behind your brand? Tell your customers and prospects about your brand, and you can nurture a lead into a sale.

Video Emails

These types of emails are similar to brand story emails. You can use them to share your expertise and brand story creatively. For example, you can share a factory tour video, company overview, and product spotlight.

Video emails are an excellent approach because over 90% of a video message is retained compared to reading text. Moreover, they get high engagement.

Review Request Emails

There is no doubt that millennials are the largest generation globally. Also, they don't make purchases before they speak to the supplier. These buyers also reference review sites and Google reviews when researching companies. Therefore, requesting reviews of your business on the review sites helps build credibility and boost your search engine results.

You can start by requesting reviews from your best and most satisfied customers. Consider including an incentive to persuade them.

EMAIL MARKETING TOOLS

You need several email marketing tools to run a successful campaign. The email tools you need include:

- **Email Service Providers** (discussed after this)
- **Email deliverability tools:** This refers to the ability of your ESP to deliver emails to your receivers' inboxes. It is wise to have an email deliverability tester in your toolbox.
- **Email testing and tracking tools**: You need to test and track your campaign's performance and create optimized iterations of your email campaigns.
- **Email personalization tools:** An email personalization tool will help you add recipients' names to your emails, among other personalization features.

HOW EMAIL MARKETING WORKS

Email marketing is a marketing approach where brands send promotional messages to people in large numbers. Brands mostly use email marketing to generate sales by nurturing leads, sharing promotional offers, or extending their content marketing efforts.

An effective email marketing strategy must have three essential elements:

An email list

This is a database of subscribers who have agreed to receive your emails. An email list is the backbone of a successful email campaign. You can use different approaches to create your email list. However, the most straightforward approach is to create a lead magnet (or an offer) your target audience would be interested in. Examples include offering coupons in exchange for their email address.

An email service provider (ESP)

An ESP or email marketing platform is software that helps brands manage their email list. It also allows you to design and implement automated email campaigns. Furthermore, using an ESP enables you to create automatic triggers whenever your audience performs specific actions.

For example, you can send a cart reminder if a user puts an item in the cart and does not pick "checkout." Such triggers allow you to personalize interactions, thus improving engagement and open rates.

Clearly defined goals

You can use email to achieve several business goals, such as:

- Enhance brand awareness
- Drive sales
- Engage customers
- Generate and nurture leads
- Boost customer loyalty and lifetime value

These three factors must align for your email marketing strategy to be effective. Begin by segmenting your email list based on subscriber actions and demographics. After that, create emails to persuade your consumers to do something. Finally, use your ESP to send emails and automatically keep an eye on your campaign.

EMAIL MARKETING STRATEGY

Various studies show that emails outperform all online marketing strategies (McDonald, 2022). An email marketing strategy forms an essential part of your marketing strategy. It is also the most economical way of promoting your products, communicating with your customers, and attaining your business goals.

Here are some of the best email marketing strategies you can implement to achieve exceptional results.

Personalize your message

This does not mean you send an individual email to each of your subscribers. Instead, it means using customer data to create a personalized message. You might want to check Amazon's emails as they are the best examples.

It is also critical to note that about 70% of brands don't personalize their emails. Therefore, using this approach will help you stand out. The most basic approach is to address your readers by name. Fortunately, most ESPs have this functionality.

- Apart from the customer's name, use the signup form to get the right information upfront. For example, request details such as location, company, and name. Just ask for the information you need.
- Also, use the actual reply-to email. Using donotreply@example.com usually takes away your messaging authenticity. Using a reply-to address improves your credibility and makes you appear more personal.
- Finally, ensure you use a genuine email signature. Use real contact information, including contact details. This allows your readers to contact you or connect with you online.

Segment your users

Segmenting your email subscribers makes your campaigns more targeted. Studies have confirmed that segmentation boosts performance (Vaughan, 2022).

Segmenting your list gives you better open rates, transactions, revenue leads, and more clients. Here are some ideas you can use with segmentation:

- **By industry:** If you offer products and services to businesses or consumers, it will help understand their industry.
- **By company size:** This is also called account-based marketing. You can use company size or annual revenue to boost your response rate.
- **By sales cycle:** Early stage buyers might not be ready for an aggressive sales pitch. But buyers who are ready to buy willingly respond to free trial offers and webinars.

Send mobile-optimized emails

Over 60% of marketing emails are opened on a mobile device (APARNA, 2022). This is a massive number that marketers must consider. It is not an excellent strategy to send an email to subscribers who read their emails on their mobile, the email is not optimized for the device. Some tips you can use include:

- **Use responsive email design (RED):** This approach ensures user experience is optimized regardless of the device used. Luckily, most ESPs offer this feature.
- **The subject line and preheader should be precise**: The subject line is critical, and you should keep it precise to make it effortless for the reader to know the email's subject.
- **Make your CTAs visible and apparent**: Mobile devices have varying sizes. Therefore, ensure you consider this by making your CTAs big, bold and effortless to click.

Test copy, design, and buttons

Testing will offer data to help you make practical decisions that can significantly improve your marketing performance. The email marketing campaign elements you should test include:

- Messaging
- Subject lines
- Design
- Call-to-action
- Personalization
- Sender name
- Landing page
- Target audience

You can do this by sending various emails in the subject line to a limited number of subscribers. These emails will reveal the subject lines that perform poorly and the ones that perform best.

Automate your email campaigns

Trigger-based emails are usually sent automatically based on user behavior. Popular trigger emails include thank you emails, welcome emails, and transactional emails. Examples of trigger emails you can use include:

- **Activation:** When a user creates an account but does not use your product within seven days, consider creating an activation campaign to send them an automated email with login information. Offer them steps on how they can get started.
- **Win-back:** Create a win-back email if your current customer's annual subscription is about to end. Send automated emails to all your customers at the end of their contracts.
- **Surprise:** You can surprise your loyal customers with freebies from time to time. Create a surprise email sent to your best customers, automatically giving them a free offer.

EMAIL MARKETING CAMPAIGN

Armed with all the above-mentioned tactics, you are ready to run an email marketing campaign. An *email marketing campaign* is a set of coordinated individual email messages deployed across a specified period with a single objective. The specific goals could be downloading a white paper, purchasing, or signing up for a webinar.

Here are some essential tips for your email marketing campaign:

Create a precise subject line

Each email should have a precise subject line, focused content, and a specific CTA to achieve the campaign's goal. Your subject line should perfectly balance between being fascinating and informative. Moreover, it should persuade users to click without over or underpromising the content.

Content should be focused

Focused content is content relevant to your email marketing campaign. It should also be relevant to your users. Most marketers use dynamic content in their email campaigns to appeal to different segments within their audience.

Include one main CTA

Effective email marketing campaigns usually have a single primary CTA. However, they also have the possibility of a secondary CTA. Therefore, your CTA buttons should be bold and clear. They should not be overwhelming or take away from your messaging.

Use ESPs

For best results, use ESPs to run your email campaigns. They make it effortless to segment your audience and personalize your messages. This approach ensures users get relevant information.

They can be a one-off or a series

Your email marketing campaign can be a one-off or a series of emails sent over a particular time frame. If you are sending multiple messages, ensure consistency in your overall concept.

KEY TAKEAWAYS

- Email marketing is an effective online marketing tool that has stood the test of time.
- Consider using an email service provider to make your email marketing more effective.
- When writing emails, consider the recipient's position in the sales funnel.
- Personalization and segmentation will go a long way in making your email marketing campaigns effective.

CHAPTER 6
WEBSITE DIGITAL MARKETING

Talking about a digital marketing strategy without mentioning website digital marketing is not practical. By now, you have gathered enough information concerning digital marketing. We will dive straight into website marketing.

WEBSITE DIGITAL MARKETING STRATEGIES

A website is an excellent marketing tool for your business. It represents your brand online and is one of the most critical digital marketing channels you can use. In this regard, every company that aspires to succeed online must have a clear-cut website marketing strategy. It is no longer optional!

Website marketing is simply promoting your website on the Internet. This is a channel you can include in your overall digital marketing strategy.

HOW WEBSITE MARKETING WORKS

You must have a solid strategy to promote your brand using your website.

Here are the essential steps you must follow:

Website design

The first step is to develop a website that accurately represents your brand. Your website acts as your online shopping window. Therefore ensure it looks good on the outside. Also, when your clients enter your online shop, they should find everything organized.

Ensure that your website:

- **Has a straightforward hierarchical structure.** Ensure all pages are accessible from your homepage in less than three clicks.
- **Is functional and user-friendly.** Get rid of any design elements that make your site challenging to navigate.
- **Has accurate information about your brand and products.** Ensure the website contains all the relevant information users might want to know. Use visual elements to grab user attention.
- **Loads fast and is mobile-optimized**. Most users can access your website from their mobile devices. Ensure they get the best experience possible.

SEO Optimization

You need a proper SEO strategy to increase your rankings and traffic from search engines like Google. SEO, or search engine optimization, is the process of enhancing your website's visibility in search engines. There are several steps, including:

- **Technical SEO:** ensures your website does not have crawl errors or any other bugs that might prevent search engines from indexing it.
- **On-page SEO:** makes your web pages SEO-friendly. It also ensures search engine crawlers can effortlessly read your content.
- **SEO content:** ensures you write content that meets user needs.
- **Off-page SEO:** involves promoting your website to get top-quality links from other websites.
- **Local SEO:** This step involves optimizing your site for local-aware searches. It helps your brand get more customers to your physical store.

Social Media Optimization

It is also critical to optimize your site for social media. You can achieve social media optimization by:

- Including visual elements on your website that you can share on social media.
- Having social media sharing buttons on the pages you would like to share on social media.
- Ensuring that when a user clicks the share button, the generated snippet is formatted well.

Create a content marketing plan

You need a solid content marketing strategy. The proper plan has five phases as outlined below:

- **Planning:** This will help you understand how to make your content unique.
- **Production:** This involves optimizing your content as you create it.
- **Promotion:** You need to know when, how, and where to publish the content.
- **Analysis:** In this phase, you monitor the performance of your content and check where to improve.
- **Amplification:** Here, you will understand the content you need to amplify to optimize your ROI. From here, you go back to the first step, and the cycle continues.

Furthermore, please begin with a keyword search for an effective content marketing strategy. This will help you discover the SEO keywords your content should target. After that, analyze your competition to find out what works for them. It also helps to analyze Google search results to find the type of content Google wants for your target keywords. Check the content length and format.

Promote your website on social media

Create business social media accounts (by now, you know how to do this) and link your website to them. You can also add links to your social media account to your website.

Use paid ads to expand your reach

It takes time for SEO to work and organically get a sizable number of social media followers. Therefore, it will help use paid advertising to accelerate the process. Paid advertising enables you to get targeted traffic fast.

The most common advertising platforms to use are:

- **Google Ads** – usually target users based on the search terms they use on Google. It also displays your ads on other Google properties like Gmail, YouTube or websites participating in Google AdSense.
- **Facebook paid ads** - allow you to promote your website using Facebook, Messenger, and Instagram.

Ensure your website and content are up-to-date

First, ensure you upgrade your website software to the latest version. Also, ensure it is secure and uses the latest technologies. After that, make sure your content is fresh and relevant. As your website grows, some content will be obsolete, which is unsuitable for search engines.

Start by looking for pages that don't have rankings, traffic, or backlinks (also known as thin content pages). You can update, remove or merge them with other pages.

DOMAIN NAME MARKETING STRATEGY

A domain name is basically a string of text that maps to a numeric IP address. This is what people use to access a website from client software. In plain English, it is the words that a user types into a browser's window to access a specific site. In business terms, it is your property!

In this sense, a domain name marketing strategy is using Internet addresses to increase the potential number of visitors to your site. It enables brands to use domains to boost the standing of their website.

Importance of domain names

You can determine a brand's success by looking at the traffic and engagement it attracts on its website. Therefore, if you don't get it right with your website, Google and Facebook Ads will not help you.

Here is why domain names are essential:

- **Brand positioning:** a well-thought-out domain name enables a brand to establish itself and what it offers.
- **First impression:** It is what you use to introduce your business. It is your first impression.
- **Marketing touchpoints:** Having a good domain name enables you to add extra zest to your digital marketing venture. For example, you can use them as touchpoints that attract and engage your audience.

HOW TO USE DOMAIN NAMES IN YOUR DIGITAL MARKETING STRATEGY

Your domain name is a very versatile marketing tool. It allows you to tailor your approach based on your goal and campaign. Here are some creative ways of using domain names in your digital marketing strategy.

Create targeted campaigns

Giving your marketing campaigns a unique identity on the Internet is an excellent way of getting the best out of your marketing campaigns. For example, you can use a unique domain name to direct users to a particular landing page. This strategy helps you:

- Generate more attention
- Target specific users
- Experiment creative ideas
- Track specific results
- Attempt different messages and gauge what performs well

Give products a unique identity

Every business usually has a star product they promote more than others. In this situation, you can give such a product its unique identity to make it shine brighter. An excellent example is what Amazon did with Kindle.

Create branded short links to boost exposure

Have you ever seen a link like bit.ly or virg.in on social media? Many people think sharing branded links on social media is costly. Branded links are ideal for boosting brand awareness. Using a branded link like pay.online/digital enhances user trust and increases click-through rates.

Harness the power of backlinks

Top-quality backlinks are critical to giving your site a good search ranking. The words on which the hyperlink is set also make backlinks more powerful. Also, when the words in the URL match those in the anchor text, it makes the link more credible.

Add a creative twist to your digital marketing campaign

A domain name helps marketers get the most out of their promotional efforts. It offers many benefits, especially with search and memorability. Ideas you can use include:

- Having a domain name for a particular season
- Location-based domain names
- Specific day
- Campaign slogan.

Follow these tips to choose a domain name:

- Keep it short
- It should be brandable, not generic
- Don't use numbers and hyphens
- Use the correct domain name extension
- Make it effortless to type
- Include keywords related to your offer
- Research

LANDING PAGES IN DIGITAL MARKETING

A landing page is a standalone web page where prospective customers can land when they click on an ad. Its objective is to capture information from your contacts in exchange for something valuable. They differ from other web pages because they are not permanently available on the website's navigation. In short, they serve a specific purpose within a particular period to a specific audience.

Once users land on the landing page, you encourage them to take action, like filling out a signup form.

Difference between landing page and homepage

Several features differentiate landing pages and homepages. For example, a home page has more links than a landing page. In addition, homepages have broader CTAs, while landing page CTAs are very specific. Lastly, people visiting your homepage have probably not decided what they want. However, users landing on the landing page have shown interest in your offer.

TYPES OF LANDING PAGES

There are different types of landing pages applicable in different scenarios. Below are the most notable types you should consider using.

Lead-gen landing pages

Lead-gen landing pages are trendy. Brands use them primarily to generate sales leads. They host ads on social media, Google, or through an email campaign urging the user to click a link to the landing page to get access to exclusive content.

Once the user lands on the landing page, the objective is to request them to share their details through a form to access the exclusive content. The landing page's CTA is the data capture form.

Single–offer landing pages

This type of landing page usually has a single asset. They rarely generate a lot of traffic to your website. But their specific nature results in more conversions.

These landing pages are effective for customers lower in the sales funnel experiencing an issue the content can address directly. Even if you don't convert them immediately, don't despair; you have their contacts and can share more content with them.

Clickthrough landing pages

This is a more immediate version of a lead-gen landing page. They are popular on eCommerce websites and focus on making fast and voluminous sales. However, they are relatively riskier because they lead prospective clients to a direct sale or subscription. On this page, clients simply click the CTA button to proceed with the transaction.

The CTA elements (buttons and links) direct users to a page where they can buy goods or services. The objective is to convert people there and then.

Hub-style landing pages

These types of landing pages usually cater to users looking for educational materials. Moreover, they organize your content in a digestible way. Use hub-style pages to:

- Gather contact details
- Educate your prospects about your brand
- Engage top-of-the-funnel prospects
- Establish your brand as a thought leader in your industry

IMPORTANCE OF LANDING PAGES

As you have already noticed, landing pages have many benefits.

The most important benefits of a landing page include:

Boosts brand credibility

Internet users love clear and straight messaging explaining the value of your offers. In this sense, having a good landing page demonstrates to your audience that you value them. You can also use landing pages to display testimonials about your products and services, which provide social proof. Social proof increases conversions.

Strengthens your brand

Maintaining a consistent style on your website's tone, copy, and appearance strengthens your brand. Even if users don't convert immediately, having a solid brand identity helps them remember you later. This increases their chances of responding to your marketing efforts and recommending you to their friends.

Critical elements of a remarkable landing page

Landing pages have different elements based on their corresponding campaign. Nonetheless, an effective landing page should have the following features.

Above the–fold content

This is the first opportunity you have to get your audience's attention. According to eye-tracking data, people want to see what is above the page fold. Therefore, ensure you:

- Include relatable images and videos.
- Address the prospect by name.
- Personalize the message to make it unique.
- Acknowledge your prospects' concerns.

CTA

Your landing page should have a CTA that aligns with the action you want your audience to take. Ensure that your CTA remains consistent throughout the landing page.

Benefit-led

Use clear, targeted, and compelling copy to showcase your unique value to your prospects. Some landing pages even include an ROI calculator to accomplish this. This approach lets your prospects predict how they can use your product to save time and cash.

Social proof

Your social page should have social proof to boost users' confidence in your products and services. You can achieve this by including:

- Stats indicating the number of new clients.
- Testimonials to help prospects see what is in it for them.
- Links to press articles or any other coverage you earned.

Closing and nurturing

Use the landing page to reiterate your message and give your prospects a clear way forward. Your goal is for your visitors to follow through on your CTA. However, they might not be ready to complete the action. You can give them a way forward by suggesting something else that can help them decide by:

- Encouraging them to join an email list
- Requesting a demo
- Downloading a report

KEY TAKEAWAYS

- A website is an essential tool for any digital marketing strategy.
- Domain names are critical to your digital marketing success.
- Creating a good landing page will also significantly affect your digital marketing campaign.

CHAPTER 7
SOCIAL MEDIA MARKETING STRATEGY

We have already covered social media platforms in great detail. However, you need a solid social media marketing strategy to be successful in social media marketing. A strategy will help you avoid posting for the sake of posting without clear goals. You need an overall social media strategy before you delve down to platform-specific goals.

YOUR SOCIAL MEDIA MARKETING STRATEGY

Ask yourself the following questions to create an overall social media strategy.

Why do you want to put your brand on social media?

Your social media goals will help you answer this question. These are the general social media goals most top brands use:

- Enhance brand awareness
- Drive traffic to the brand website
- Offer social customer support
- Generate new leads
- Build a community around the brand
- Follow conversations about the brand

- Increase sales and sign-ups hence growing revenue
- Increase brand engagement
- Boost press mentions

What audience are you targeting?

Understanding your target audience makes it effortless for you to determine what, where and when you are going to post. In this regard, you need to create marketing personas. You can use different approaches to develop personas. However, the most common style is to use the 5Ws and 1H.

- **Who is your target audience?** Specify their age, gender, location, job title, and salary.
- **What can you provide that they are interested in?** For example, educational content, entertainment, new product reviews, etc.
- **Where are they mostly found online?** Is it Facebook, Twitter, Instagram, or other niche platforms?
- **When do they search for the type of content you can offer?** For instance, during the daily commute or on the weekend.
- **Why do they consume this type of content?** To live a healthier life, improve their job or stay up-to-date with something.
- **How do they consume the content?** Is it by reading social media posts or watching videos?

What will you share?

We are not talking about the content you will share here. Instead, we are talking about themes. If you scroll through the social media platforms of notable players in your industry, you will discover they have a consistent theme.

For instance, if a company sells men's underwear, the company can share photos from their customers and pictures of their products. You need several themes to allow you to share a wide range of content to keep your audience engaged without appearing vague.

Your personas will help you decide on the most appropriate theme. For instance, you can choose a theme based on their challenges and goals and how your brand can help them solve those challenges.

Where will you share your content?

You must then decide where you will share the content. Remember, you don't have to be on all social media platforms. However, it would help to have a complete business profile on Facebook, Twitter, Instagram, and LinkedIn. These profiles will always appear on Google's first page of search results when people search your brand.

Understanding your target audience will help you make the right choice. Consider a social media platform where your target audience is active. Also, your brand's X factor will help you decide. For instance, if you have great photos and videos, Instagram would suit you.

When will you share?

It is also critical to determine when you will share your content. Here, you have to look at your target audience's behaviors. Some things that can guide you include:

- Sports fans usually visit social media before, during, and immediately after a game.
- Athletes usually go on social media to cool down after their workout.
- People that love traveling are likely to be active on social media during weekends or when planning their next trip.
- Nursing mothers could be scrolling their phones at midnight while breastfeeding.

HOW ARE YOU GOING TO IMPLEMENT THE STRATEGY? – YOUR SOCIAL MEDIA MARKETING PLAN

A strategy informs you where you are going. However, you need a plan of how you will get there! Your plan will tell you how to fill out your social media profiles and the tone you will use.

How to create a social media marketing content plan

As mentioned above, you need to plan how to deliver relevant social media content consistently. Here are seven critical steps to create an operational plan:

#1: Understand how your prospects move from awareness to conversion

Here, you'll go beyond your personas. You need to offer your audience an experience they'll fall in love with. Put yourself in their shoes and ask yourself:

- What comes to their mind first when they are researching a product?
- How do they proceed from there?
- What's the last question they ask before making a purchase?

Your target customers are usually asking different questions. That way, you can build brand trust by providing valuable content that answers these questions. The content can be in the form of webinars, infographics, images, videos, or blog posts.

#2: Decide why you will use social media for your business and identify KPIs

Define your social media goals to help you assess success and failure. We have already covered this at the beginning of this chapter. With your goals defined, you need metrics to help you measure your growth. Additionally, your goal(s) will determine your KPIs.

#3: Select a social network to engage your audience

By now, you understand how the major social networks work and know which is best for your brand.

#4: Research Content topics

After selecting the right social network, plan your content. Your content should be relevant, specific, and unique. Ensure you create content that will engage your target audience.

You can run a Twitter poll or create a questionnaire to get feedback from your audience on the kind of content they would like. Google Forms is an excellent free tool you can use to create professional questionnaires. You can also monitor your competitors and find inspiration from what works for them.

#5: Prepare your content calendar

The first step is deciding the target customer for which the content is designed. After that, choose a topic (ensure your subjects are industry-specific).

Use transactional, informational, and navigational keywords to create blog article titles. Transactional keywords attract people looking for the best or cheapest. Informational keywords talk about what and how. They establish you as an expert. Finally, navigational keywords help people find what they are looking for. They usually include a brand name.

Finally, have an outline of the content for each section. The rule of thumb breaks typical blog content into four sections:

- Introduction
- Body
- Conclusion
- Call to action

After that, create a content plan having the following sections:

- Publish date
- Title/Description
- Status
- Due date
- Type of content
- Producer/designer
- Editor

#6: Engage consistently to build trust

You must engage your users in two-way conversations to establish yourself as a thought leader. Moreover, your audience will feel safer if you engage them on social media for customer support.

#7: Measure progress and make necessary adjustments

The final step of your social media marketing plan is measuring success. You need a formula to determine whether your efforts are bearing fruit. Here are the three main success indicators:

Conversions

Conversions will show you whether you are driving sales from social media. A social media dashboard can make it effortless to analyze conversions more efficiently.

Reach

This is the number of people your content has affected. This metric enables you to gauge how well your social media content resonates with your target audience. Some indicators include:

- Twitter followers
- LinkedIn connections
- website visitors
- Likes on Facebook
- Instagram followers
- YouTube channel subscribers

Engagement

You also need to monitor engagement. This shows you how many people are interacting with you online. Metrics to measure include:

- Clicks on your posts
- Mentions and retweets
- Shares on social media
- Comments on your posts

Why you need a social media strategy

There are six main reasons why brands should formulate their social media marketing strategy before taking their brands to social media platforms. Here are the benefits of having a social media strategy:

- **It helps build a robust, organic presence:** A solid strategy will help you plan in advance, enabling you to be on social media consistently. Without consistency, your social media account will not grow.
- **It saves time:** Having a social media strategy helps you to save time. For example, having everything scheduled for a whole month reduces the time you spend posting daily.
- **It ensures you cover your goals:** Having a strategy ensures your efforts are fruitful and support your broader business goals.
- **It allows you to target your audience effectively:** Part of the social media strategy might include using audience engagement elements like polls and questionnaires. These approaches help you understand your audience's pain points better.
- **It leaves you room to be creative:** A strategy will highlight the methods, elements, and networks that work best for your brand. This facilitates the creation of content that resonates with your audience. It also allows you to refine your content and be more creative.
- **It helps you stay ahead of the competition:** One of the greatest benefits of having a social media strategy is that it makes you efficient. When you follow all the tips, you are likely to be ahead of your competition.

THE 70-20-10 RULE FOR SOCIAL MEDIA MARKETING

You can apply the 70-20-10 rule to your social media marketing strategy. While any business can use this rule, it works best for new companies that need to kickstart and are unsure about what to post.

The rule states:

- **70% of your content should include brand-building content:** This refers to content that establishes your brand as an expert in the industry. It can be videos, slideshows, or infographics demonstrating your knowledge and expertise.
- **20% of your content should include posts from trusted sources you shared:** This saves you the hustle of having to create new content consistently. It is important only to share content from trusted sources. Moreover, the content should be valuable and interesting to

your audience. Always ensure your content is relevant to your target audience.

- **10% should be self-promotional content, such as links to your blog or websites:** These are posts that encourage people to share your content or subscribe. Ensure you include a clear call to action in these types of posts.

This rule will enable you to create connections with prospects while also engaging them at a personal level.

KEY TAKEAWAYS

- If you fail to create a social media marketing strategy, you are planning to fail.
- An implementation plan should accompany your social media strategy to be complete.
- If you follow the tips on social media marketing strategy, you will likely stay ahead of the competition.
- The 70-20-10 rule is an excellent way of handling your content.

CHAPTER 8
SEO AND SOCIAL MEDIA MARKETING

Search engine optimization is essential when it comes to digital marketing. Social media platforms have changed their algorithms, making it a bit challenging to get organic results from social media. Creating excellent content takes time, and many small businesses don't have to spare.

However, social media is not a bulletin board where your brand posts articles and images to promote its products and services. The ultimate goal of your social media presence should be to drive traffic to your website.

WHAT IS SOCIAL MEDIA SEO?

Social media SEO, also known as social SEO, combines social media and SEO strategies to boost your position in search results, conversions, and website traffic (Berg, 2022). You can also define social media as using social media platforms as an indirect tool to boost a brand's search visibility and ranking in organic searches (Greene, 2021).

Social media does not directly impact SEO. However, social signals such as shares, likes, and comments, generated by people interacting with your content on social media platforms have an indirect effect. For example, interaction helps to build customer loyalty and boost brand exposure and awareness, which indirectly helps to enhance your online traffic and visibility.

WHY SOCIAL MEDIA IS IMPORTANT IN SEO

The impact of social media on SEO is not straightforward. For instance, Bing's Webmaster Guidelines confirm that Bing ranks pages with more shares higher than those with fewer shares. Google has also confirmed that social media is not a direct ranking factor.

However, several studies claim there is a connection between social shares and rankings. Be that as it may, correlation does not mean causation. Therefore, it might not be correct to say that social shares impact rankings.

Here is how social media indirectly affects SEO:

Increased visibility

Quality backlinks are essential for higher rankings on Google and boosting domain authority. For example, if your audience engages with your social media content by sharing it, it boosts visibility. Consequently, the increased visibility means more people are likely to find and read your posts. Moreover, it increases inbound links to your website, enhances your credibility, and shows your content's popularity.

Furthermore, increased credibility is excellent for SEO. For example, promoting your content on social media allows bloggers to link to your content from their sites. It also helps you earn links from multiple sources. Therefore, social media increases your brand's visibility, earning you more links that are good for SEO.

Boost SEO Ranking signals

While shares are not a ranking factor, time on page and site is. Therefore, it is correct to say social media helps SEO by enabling you to improve metrics that impact rankings. Social media increases traffic to your search-optimized pages, which improves your visibility and engagement on social media. If you target the right people on social media with relevant content, they will likely stay on your website longer.

This is critical because Google's ranking algorithm considers the length of every interaction on your site. Therefore, you can use highly targeted social media posts to increase the average time people spend on your website. Consequently, that can boost search rankings eventually.

Social media posts get your content indexed quicker

You can use social media platforms to get your pages indexed by Google quicker. When you post new content on your website, you immediately start sharing it on Twitter, Facebook, and LinkedIn to get clicks on it. This alerts Google that there is a page that needs to be crawled and re-indexed.

Social interaction data helps improve your SEO content

Interaction data such as click-through rates on SERPs, time on page, bounce rates, and time on site are what search engines use to rank content. Therefore, you can use your brand's social community as a sounding board to test different content. For example, you can look for your social media posts with the best engagement and use those insights to structure your page titles and descriptions.

If people click on a social media post, they are highly likely to click on the article if they see it on SERPs. In short, use the social interaction data from your social media dashboard to improve your SEO title and meta description. This data will also help you decide on the topic clusters you should be building out.

Social media builds search demand

Social media posts help direct new visitors to your website, boosting your website's visibility. For instance, if you build your brand awareness using a social media platform, many people who know you will search for your brand name.

Consequently, you will be able to rank multiple pieces of content on Google's first page even if your site has fewer backlinks. Therefore, when you increase your content's visibility and coverage, your social media presence amplifies your Google presence with search queries connected to your brand.

Social media enables you to identify your audience for your SEO content

One of the most significant advantages of social media is that it allows you to learn about your audience. Once you have your prospects' profiles, you will know their general tendencies. For example, where they go online and what they are looking for.

This information makes it effortless for you to find keywords to target that are relevant to the people most likely to do business with you. Also, creating blog posts that target specific demographics on social media helps you refine your SEO strategy.

Social media helps with keyword research

Social media is an excellent place to follow trends and discover new keyword opportunities for your content and profile. This shows you what people want to read about and follow, which can help you to rank higher. Consider posting "ask the expert" posts on your social media pages to boost engagement and to discover new ideas for long-tail Q&A keywords relevant to your customers.

HOW TO EFFECTIVELY COMBINE SEO AND SOCIAL MEDIA

If you use social media correctly, it will boost your SEO strategy. Here are some tips you can use to combine SEO and social media effectively:

Amplify content to facilitate indexing and ranking

By the way, Google owes nothing! Google is not obliged to index your website and display it on page one, even for searches with your company name. Fortunately, social media can help you amplify your content. For example, when you share pages and posts on social media, they will get traffic despite their ranking on Google. This increases the chances of Google noticing the pages. This can result in faster indexing and opportunities to rank higher.

Brand awareness

While SEO enables users to find your website through organic keyword strategies, social media works better. For example:

- You can use hashtags to help your posts and profiles get discovered, which entices people to follow your business.
- Comment on relevant posts on behalf of your brand to boost your visibility with people engaging with that post.
- Encourage happy customers to tag you in posts about your products or services to increase your visibility.

- You can also use influencer marketing to amplify your business with their massive following.

Build trust in your brand

Trust in your business is critical for growth. For example, social proof through reviews, statistics, and testimonials can help build your brand's trust. Additionally, you can also use how-to posts to demonstrate your expertise and share them on social media to boost traffic. Use social media platforms to humanize your brand and make it more authentic.

Use social media to boost link-building

Despite the dynamic nature of the SEO landscape, backlinks will always play a critical role in your ranking. When other websites link to your website, it gives a nod of approval to Google. However, social media does not provide you with backlinks. Combining brand awareness and content amplification driven by social media can result in more backlinks. Any individual or business that interacts with your social media content is a potential link about to happen.

Social media enhances local SEO

The hospitality, entertainment, and dining industries can benefit significantly from local SEO. It is also helpful for small businesses having physical shops. It helps for your business to appear on page one when someone in your locality is seeking your service.

In this sense, name, address, and phone number (NAP) are essential for local SEO because proximity to the searcher is an important ranking factor. Social media profiles offer you an additional place to publish your NAP details for Google to check. You can also use social media posts to post local hashtags, location tags, and local keywords. Moreover, your Google Business Profile also works as an arm of social media where you can publish posts.

Bottom Line

Success in SEO and social media starts with great content. Excellent and unique content that results in remarkable social media and SEO performance. The hallmark of social media is engagement with people. Therefore, the more you engage, the more likely you are to rank higher because people and search engines love you!

KEY TAKEAWAYS

- SEO is critical when it comes to digital marketing.
- Strategic use of social media for your business can significantly help your SEO strategy and help your business rank high on SERPs.
- Content remains a critical aspect of both SEO and social media strategies.

CHAPTER 9
MEASUREMENT - SOCIAL MEDIA DATA MANAGEMENT

In your social media campaign, social media analytics and campaign measurement tools provide critical strategic marketing information. Since a lot of consumer information is shared on social media daily, social listening tools are crucial in analyzing your audience and competitive and productive research. The essence of social media analytics is collecting and analyzing marketing and audience data to inform business decisions.

SOCIAL MEDIA ANALYTICS

Social media analytics is collecting and analyzing data points from social media platforms to help inform your social media strategy and improve engagement around your social media posts, whether paid or organic. Understand how to fulfill their demands.

Social media analytics will help you determine whether your strategy is working. It will also help you determine whether:

- You know the social media trends relevant to your space.
- You can quantify the ROI you are bringing in with each campaign or post.

- You know the expectation of your audience and what they want from your content and messaging.

Why is social media analytics essential?

Before looking at the specific metrics brands need to analyze, it is essential to consider why social media analytics is critical.

It helps to measure and prove ROI and marketing impact

Analytics provide instant feedback about your company's performance on social media channels. It also enables you to determine whether your strategy is working. Suppose your plan is not working, then the data analysis will show you exactly where you need to make adjustments. The goal is to catch any downward turns quickly and correct them immediately.

It helps brands make better strategic and business decisions

Robust social media analytics will provide you with data and insights that will help you determine what is working and what is not. Besides that, it also provides critical insights that inform your overall strategic decisions. Here is how social media analytics can help you improve your decision-making:

- **Social listening:** Social listening tools will enable you to perform competitive and audience analysis.
- **Timely response in a convenient way:** Analytics give you access to real-time data, allowing you to rapidly act on more prominent trends and get ahead of your competition.
- **Minimizes business risk:** There is data to steer you down the right strategic path, showing you the right direction.

It helps you compare your performance on social media against competitors

Social media analytics allows you to monitor your competitor's performance. It also allows you to gauge your brand's performance against the average industry performance. Context is essential; therefore, you must measure success by comparing your performance to your competitors. Benchmarking gives you important insights and enables you to determine how you can stack up against the competition.

Enables you to track your marketing team's efficiency

You need an overview of your team's efficiency. Velocity is important to guide them in the right direction. Continue to work on velocity and eliminate bottlenecks in areas such as customer support that allow you to measure community management KPIs such as audience sentiment.

SOCIAL MEDIA METRICS

A business needs to track the right metrics. This is usually not as straightforward as it sounds because the world of social media metrics can be confusing. What metrics are you tracking? Are they important to your business?

Here, we'll look at the most fundamental metrics that every brand should pay attention to. These metrics are generalized across all social media platforms. Note that the names of important metrics might vary across different channels.

Your social media goals will inform your metrics. For every goal, you must have a metric to help determine whether your social strategy is achieving its goals. For example:

- **Business goal:** increase conversations.
- **Social media goal:** increase conversations from those who visit your site via posts that form part of your strategy.
- **Strategy:** increase conversions from social by 25% in the next three months.
- **Plan:** run a campaign with ads, influencers, and product tags.
- **Metric:** look at the social traffic and conversion rate.

Every social media platform has its native analytics for brands to dive into. For example, Facebook has the Insights tab, while Twitter has Twitter Analytics. If you are starting out on a low budget, you can use these native tools. However, you will need a social media analytics tool that fits your budget to minimize the time it takes to pull the metrics from different sources.

Here are the primary metrics to measure:

Engagement: Clicks, comments, likes, and shares

You can use the engagement rate metric to track how actively involved your audience is with your content and how effective your brand campaigns are. Engaged consumers will interact with your brand through interactions like social sharing, comments, and likes.

You can measure engagement by examining how many audience accounts interact with your content and how often they do it. Each network provides a native engagement metric that sums up smaller engagement opportunities such as shares, likes, and comments. High engagement rates show your audience's responsiveness and how many of them are your "real" followers.

Engagement metrics include:

- Likes, comments, and retweets
- Post engagement rate
- Account mentions

It is advisable to look at a combination of metrics to discover the levers you can pull to achieve specific goals. However, you can also use one metric to help you be more agile and turn your strategy quickly.

Awareness: Impressions & reach

Many brands frequently use this metric, but they also confuse it. Impressions and reach are critical metrics to track, primarily if your social goals revolve around brand perception and awareness. However, it is important to know the difference between impressions and reach.

At the post level, impressions refer to the number of times a post shows up in a person's timeline. "Reach" refers to the potential unique viewers a post could have. It is your follower counts and accounts that share your post's follower counts.

Although impressions can tell you a lot about your content's potential for visibility, it is essential to look at other metrics to get the ultimate performance context. For example, if you have multiple goals of boosting awareness and educating your audience, look at a combination of impressions and engagement.

A post having high impressions but low engagement was not attractive enough for audiences to act after seeing it in their feed. If a post has a high reach count and engagement rate, it is highly likely that the content went viral through shares.

Share of voice: Volume and sentiment

Share of voice is a metric typically used in public relations or as part of a paid advert campaign or competitive analysis. It shows you how much of the online space your brand occupies. Improving your share of voice is an ongoing goal that you can measure by benchmarking over time. Campaigns will come and go, but your brand will be there forever. Since you are not the only brand in your industry, it will be challenging to maintain the biggest share of voice. However, you can track its flow over time and consider the factors for the changes.

ROI: Referrals & conversions

This metric is suitable for companies that have eCommerce platforms or websites where conversions and referral traffic impact sales and marketing goals. Referrals are how a user lands on your brand's site. Web analytics breaks referrals down into sources. Here, the source you will be monitoring is "Social." "Conversions" refer to when a prospect purchases something from your site. In this sense, a social conversion is someone who visited via a social media platform and bought something during the same visit.

Click-through rates work hand in hand with referrals and conversions in ads and posts. CTRs usually compare the number of times a user clicks on your content to the number of impressions you get. In short, the number of times people viewed the ad. For example, a high CTR means the ad was effective. Remember, CTRs differ significantly across industries, content types, and networks. Common areas where brands measure CTR include:

- PPC advertisements
- Social media advertising
- Email links and CTA buttons
- On-site elements such as images and buttons

Customer care: Response rate & time

It is also important to monitor your customer experience with your brand. Moreover, it is also critical to measure your own performance. Brands need to monitor their social managers to ensure they are performing well.

In this regard, metrics like response time and response rate are critical. They enable you to track how fast your team responds to important messages and how many of them you respond to. If you operate multi-user accounts, ensure you track how much each person is doing.

Social media analytics requires the right tool. However, not many businesses utilize these important tools. Instead, they mostly use native tools that don't provide comprehensive performance metrics.

SOCIAL MEDIA ANALYTICS TOOLS

As mentioned earlier, social media platforms come with native analytics tools. However, collating the data from different social media platforms might be cumbersome. You need a tool that can benefit your campaign without being burdensome.

Sprout Social

Sprout Social is arguably the best cross-channel social media analytics tool. You can effortlessly check your performance on a single network or compare results across different networks simultaneously. For example, you can use it to track Facebook Page impressions, measure Instagram follower growth, tally Twitter link clicks and evaluate LinkedIn engagement.

Moreover, you can quickly organize and share data with straightforward presentation-ready reports. You can also use Premium Analytics to generate custom reports tailored to your brand's KPIs. Sprout provides all the important analytics at your fingertips. It also has advanced listening tools to provide valuable data related to industry influencers, audience demographics, the share of voice, and campaign performance.

HubSpot

HubSpot's analytical tools help brands tie their social media performance to business and revenue growth. The analytical tools provide expansive graphs and visuals that break down the numbers by features such as impressions, session lengths, and audience.

HubSpot also has Marking Hub, their all-in-one inbound marketing software. As a result, using the tool allows you to gain insights into the entire customer journey. This will enable you to see the marketing strategies that are working and their effect on your bottom line.

Awario

Awario is a powerful social media marketing tool that offers excellent analytics elements. Its notable features include:

- It analyzes your brand's online mentions to provide stats on reach and mention growth.
- It also offers a list of languages and locations with your brand mentions.
- The tool also analyzes people on social media platforms using your brand and industry keywords.
- It also provides a list of social media influencers in your niche.

Create alerts for your brand and competitors to get the most out of the tool. This will enable you to receive a step-by-step comparison of your social media performance against that of your competitors.

The tool also displays a "share of voice" graph to show how much "online buzz" your brand generates compared to your main competitors.

Snaplytics

This is an ideal tool for brand marketing on Instagram and Snapchat. It provides comprehensive performance data on the two platforms, including insights on stories and general follower growth. Moreover, the app enables you to see the best acquisition methods. The tool will also show you what causes engagement level spikes and falls, helping you optimize your platform strategy. The tool will also help you create custom reports and export the data to a CSV file.

Squarelovin

This is an analytics tool that works specifically for Instagram. It helps you track likes and followers, review post-performance, and measure general profile engagement. The tool also highlights the best time to post, filters to use, and hashtags. Furthermore, it provides your posts' history, breaking them down by hour. It will also provide insights into your audience's interests and preferences.

KEY TAKEAWAYS

- Measuring your performance is a vital part of your social media marketing strategy.
- Your social media marketing goals will inform the metrics you use.
- You can use native metrics or third-party tools for better and less cumbersome results.
- Get a tool that can help you measure the metrics that interest you.

CHAPTER 10

STEP-BY-STEP GUIDE TO CREATING A SOCIAL MEDIA MARKETING STRATEGY

You've already learned a lot concerning social media marketing. This chapter brings it all together in this step-by-step guide to creating your social media marketing strategy. A strategy has more benefits than just guiding your marketing strategy. Having a well-thought-out strategy will:

- Ensure you remain on course as you pursue your goals
- Be an essential resource for new team members
- Help your marketing team design social media content
- Enable you to keep your marketing consistent on multiple social media platforms
- Allow you to generate search engine optimized (SEO) content.

Creating your brand's social media strategy offers you an upper hand over your competitors because your marketing will be more thoughtful, data-driven, and effortless to create.

Follow these steps to create a successful social media marketing strategy:

Step 1: Establish your "why" and set objectives

The first thing is to state what you want to achieve with your social media campaign. The best approach is to outline a goal and several objectives.

Don't confuse the two: a goal represents your why while objectives are the milestones that mark your progression towards the goal.

To determine your goal, ask yourself why you want to pursue social media marketing. Examples of goals can be:

- Improve brand awareness
- Increase website traffic
- Boost revenue
- Generate leads
- Respond to customer questions and comments

Note that you don't have to restrict yourself to one goal or objective. You are free to go for as many targets as is realistically possible.

Step 2: Identify your target audience

Who are the people you are targeting to reach on social media? This is a critical question that will shape the rest of your strategy. It helps you to have a better understanding of how you will market your brand. You probably have an idea of your audience. However, it will help if you create a marketing persona to help you when creating content.

Here is how to create a marketing persona:

Question	Possible Answers
What does your ideal customer look like?	<ul><li>What do they do when they're free?</li><li>Are they a start-up or a fortune 500?</li><li>What are their revenues?</li><li>How old are the decision makers?</li><li>Are they financially stable or struggling?</li></ul>
What would persuade them to buy?	<ul><li>What are their most significant pain points?</li><li>What gaps do they want to fill?</li><li>What are they struggling with most?</li><li>What solutions are they currently paying for? Are they happy?</li></ul>
What is the outlook of their buying process?	<ul><li>Do they seem to be ready?</li><li>How much do you need to convince them?</li><li>Are you targeting managers, employees, or someone else?</li><li>How many decision-makers are involved?</li><li>What roles would they play in the buying process?</li></ul>
How can you get your brand in front of them?	<ul><li>Do they love reading, watching, or listening?</li><li>On which social analysis platform do decision makers spend their time?</li><li>How do they prefer to consume content?</li><li>Are they on their workstation or on the go?</li></ul>

Step 3: Analyze your competition

After defining your target audience, it's time to look at your competition. Perform a competitive analysis to help you scrutinize your competitors' social media strategy. Check what is working and what is not. Consider looking at up to five competitors for best results. During your analysis, look at the following:

- The social media platforms they are using
- How frequently do they post
- The type of content that performs best
- How long have they been on social media
- Types of posts they use

- The comments, likes, and shares they get
- How they have presented their bio
- How do they approach their comments section and CTAs?

Take a few weeks to analyze your competition because social media performance usually fluctuates.

Step 4: Choose a suitable platform and set up your brand profiles

The next step is to select the social media channels you will use based on your findings from the previous steps. By now, you know the top-performing social media platforms and how they work.

Step 5: Build a content calendar

A content calendar is a timeline that will outline when you will publish and the contents of each post. It will also help you be consistent in your posting, and a calendar will help you with that. Include different content types in your calendar.

The best practice is to plan at least a month ahead. This approach allows you to develop posts that are unique and consistent. It will also help you if you plan to work with influencers because they need a few weeks to work on their social media goals. Don't forget to create an approval process that ensures all your posts meet your quality standards.

Step 6: Start publishing

Start with posts welcoming new followers. You can also post content introducing your brand, products, and services to your audience. It will take some time to build a community of followers. You have already learned how to do that for different social media platforms.

Step 7: Analyze results and adjust strategy

Your social media strategy should not be set in stone. Treat it as a working document and adjust where and when necessary. For example, as your brand grows, you will have to update your objectives, target audience, and content calendar.

Based on the platforms you are using, you will measure different metrics. Luckily, you have already learned about this. Use the data you collect to refine your strategy.

CURRENT TRENDS IN SOCIAL MEDIA MARKETING

One of the things we have mentioned continually from the beginning of this book is looking at best practices by top brands. Here are the ones that matter the most at the moment:

#1: TikTok has become the most important social network for marketing

Over the past few years, Instagram has been marketers' number one social media platform. However, TikTok reached the 1 billion user mark in 2021, making it the 7th most popular social media platform globally (Mikolajczyk, 2021). Additionally, Google Search Trends indicate that TikTok dominates Instagram's short-form video content.

Reports also show that the search demand for TikTok has grown by 173% (Tien & Prodanovic, 2022). However, many brands are still hesitant to invest in the platform. You can go ahead with your competition and create your TikTok account.

#2: Smaller networks and bigger ad dollars

Studies have revealed that consumers have become more receptive to advertising on "smaller" platforms like Snapchat, Pinterest and TikTok than on perceived bigger social networks. Additionally, TikTok ads are leading this charge.

In smaller networks, users are less likely to suffer ad fatigue, making them more effective. Pinterest, TikTok and Snapchat also encourage brands to make ads that fit in with organic content being posted by regular users.

#3: Shoppers expect to buy directly on social media

According to eMarketers, social commerce will grow into an $80 billion industry by 2025. Around 81% of shoppers use social media to discover new brands and research products (McLachlan & Gurr, 2022). Also, many brands have realized that allowing these users to go to the checkout in the same app is sensible.

Moreover, most social media platforms have in-app shopping solutions, and others are working to join the fold. While social commerce will not replace eCommerce anytime soon, it is a trend worth checking out.

#4: No one wants to talk to your brand on the phone

A survey commissioned by Facebook revealed that 64% of people prefer messages to calls. Other experts suggest that by 2023 over 60% of customer support requests will be handled digitally (Omale, 2021). Therefore, you can consider this trend while creating your social media strategy.

#5: Long-form video is not working, except on YouTube

If you are active on social media, you'll discover that most videos published on the Internet are short. That's why all the top social media platforms have a feature for presenting short videos. For instance, Instagram Reels and YouTube Shorts have become very popular. You should incorporate these content forms into your content strategy.

#6: Creator economy on the rise

Creator refers to professional influencer marketers and amateur content creators. Social media platforms have created tools to help brands harness the power of Creators. For example, Twitter has paid "Super Followers," Instagram has "Collabs," and TikTok has "Creator Marketplace." Take advantage of these features to add value to your content.

CHAPTER 11
AFFILIATE MARKETING – A STEP-BY-STEP GUIDE

Affiliate marketing is one of the most misunderstood concepts in the world of digital marketing. According to Google Trends, there is a continued rise in interest in affiliate marketing globally. However, that does not mean that affiliate marketing is easy or a get-rich-quick scheme! It is a tricky business venture that requires having the right strategy. That's where this chapter comes in.

WHAT IS AFFILIATE MARKETING?

Affiliate marketing is a performance-based marketing strategy where a retailer, usually an online one, rewards a website with a commission for every client referred through the website's promotional activities. In essence, it involves a retailer paying a small commission to people referred to as affiliates who recommend their products and services to others. It mainly consists of sending traffic to a retailer's website and receiving a commission when your referrals buy the product or service you recommended/

Four parties are involved in this process:

- **The merchant:** the company that produces or sells the product or service. The merchant hopes to maximize sales by calling upon other people to help them promote their goods or services. Having an extensive network of affiliates promoting your product is a significant source of traffic and sales.
- **The affiliate:** the person/brand promoting the product or service. They receive a small commission every time someone buys a recommended product or service.
- **Affiliate networks:** Internet-based networks where merchants list their affiliate programs.
- **The consumer:** the people affiliates recommend products or services to and end up buying. These are the most important people in the entire process. The affiliate needs to use highly relevant content to convince them to buy.

Affiliate purchase is a process that involves several steps:

1. The affiliate displays an advertisement for a merchant on their website, blog, or video.
2. One of their users clicks the links from where the affiliate has displayed it.
3. The user then makes a purchase on the affiliate site.
4. Since the link is unique to the affiliate, the transaction is recorded against them.
5. The merchant pays the affiliate a proportion of the sale value.

HOW AFFILIATE MARKETING WORKS

Affiliate marketing payment models

Mostly, affiliates earn a commission each time one of their visitors clicks through to a merchant's site and purchases a product. However, there are many other affiliate marketing models you might encounter:

- **Pay-Per-Sale (PPS):** in this model, the merchant pays the affiliate for each sale they generate.
- **Pay-Per-Lead (PPL):** here, the merchant pays the affiliate for every lead generated, for instance, trial creations, online form submissions, pre-purchases, and free demo sign-ups.
- **Pay-Per-Click (PPC):** in this model, the merchant pays the affiliate for all clicks/traffic they generate, even if the visitor does not turn into a lead.

Most affiliate programs use the PPS model, meaning affiliates get paid when their referrals buy a product or service they recommend.

Keeping track of affiliate marketing traffic

Most merchants use traffic tracking software to attribute sales. Here is how it works:

When an affiliate signs up for an affiliate program, they are given a unique ID which they add at the end of all their links for the program. This unique ID will tell the merchant every time you send traffic to them.

However, the system is not foolproof. An affiliate can send traffic to a partner's website, but they don't make a purchase immediately. Instead, they return to the merchant's site later and pay up. Is the affiliate still responsible for the sale? Different programs handle such cases differently. Therefore, the affiliate must understand how a program works before joining.

When do affiliates get paid?

This also depends on the affiliate program. However, the trend is that merchants pay weekly or monthly. Furthermore, some programs have payout thresholds meaning you can only withdraw money when you attain a certain amount in your balance.

Expenses for affiliate marketers

Every affiliate needs good quality hosting that can handle a lot of traffic. Therefore, their first expense is a website where they will publish content, make recommendations and build a following. The website attracts the following expenses:

- Hosting
- Domain name
- Website design or theme
- Development costs
- Maintenance costs

Affiliates also need an audience for their content to generate any traffic and affiliate income. In this regard, they need search engine optimization, PPC, social media, and other inbound marketing approaches. All of these cost money.

AFFILIATE MARKETING: STEP-BY-STEP

Affiliate marketing might seem straightforward. But the implementation process is usually relatively complex. Here is what an affiliate marketer needs:

- **Planning:** Every successful affiliate marketing strategy starts with far-reaching planning.
- **Building your site:** The affiliate has to develop their website, define their niche and create their domain name.
- **Set up analytics:** After that, they must implement analytics and decide their KPIs to enable them to measure and improve their performance.
- **Choose programs:** Select the affiliate programs you will be working with and sign up for them.
- **Create content:** Create affiliate content recommending the products or services you have signed up with.
- **Build an audience:** Promote your content and build your search presence to generate enough traffic that you can earn affiliate income.
- **Achieve profitability:** Ensure your income is more than what you spend on your affiliate marketing strategy. It should also be enough to cover the time you invest.
- **Maximize performance:** Optimize your website and affiliate marketing strategy to get the most out of your affiliate programs.

- **Scale your strategy:** Your strategy should allow you to experiment with new methods to enable you to expand your audience and revenue.
- **Automate everything you can:** This will help maximize your profit while reducing your manual workload.

HOW TO BECOME AN AFFILIATE MARKETER

Every successful affiliate marketer must have the following:

- A collection of products to review, mention or recommend within their regular content.
- Platforms where they will recommend products and services such as email, YouTube, or blog.
- A large enough audience that can generate serious affiliate income.
- An effective affiliate marketing strategy.

Plan

To start on the right note, you must plan. In your plan, ensure you know the following:

- The budget you will work with
- The affiliate income you will make
- How much profit do you need, and when will you reach profitability
- The number of affiliate sales you need to hit your target
- The traffic you need to hit your target
- The KPIs and metrics you need to track.

Choose product

Consider promoting products you already know and are passionate about. This will ensure you can discuss the product in enough detail to make valid recommendations. A good approach would be to choose products in your niche.

Search affiliate networks

An affiliate network will save merchants time searching for affiliates and the affiliate's time hunting for merchants. Popular affiliate networks include Amazon Associates, Clickbank, and Shareasale. If you are starting, you can conduct a manual search before you start using affiliate networks.

Choose platforms to post affiliate content

After selecting your affiliate program, you need a place to post the link. Fortunately, you have already learned how all these platforms work. They include:

- Blog or website
- Email marketing
- YouTube
- Social platforms including Facebook, Pinterest, Instagram, TikTok, and Snapchat.

Use the knowledge you've gained from reading the book to select the right platform for your affiliate marketing strategy.

Build an audience large enough for affiliate marketing

We have also covered this in detail throughout the book. Therefore, you now know how to build an audience on different platforms. Nonetheless, here is a recap:

- Create affiliate content suitable for your niche by having the following features:

  ○ Consider the needs of your audience

  ○ Knowledgeable enough to give prospects advice

  ○ Genuine and trustworthy

  ○ In-depth

  ○ Critical

  ○ Useful

○ Accessible

○ Gets results

Build organic search presence

People go to search engines to search for solutions. It is critical to have your site appear regularly at the top of search pages for these queries to generate considerable traffic. Luckily, you have already learned how different algorithms work and how to fulfill their demands.

Promote your content with PPC ads

Building a search presence online usually takes time. In this sense, you need to use paid advertising to accelerate the process. The PPC ad you use depends on the platform you are using. Nonetheless, experts suggest that email marketing is the best channel for this.

Drive traffic from social media

Social media will play a significant role when building your audience. Choose the right network for your strategy for the best results. You already know eight of the best social media networks and how to use them.

Network with other sites

Reach out to publishers to whom your content is relevant to their audience. If they publish your content on their websites, it will expose you to an entirely new audience.

Maximize your affiliate marketing income

It is critical to note that affiliate marketing income usually hits a plateau. You should optimize your strategy to get the best out of each performance and maximize profits.

Essential metrics and KPIs for affiliate marketing

- Profit
- Return on investment
- Total income: your total affiliate income.
- Spend: individual expenses such as content, freelancer, and ad fees.

- Effective earnings per click (eEPC): how much you earn per click of each affiliate link.
- Payout: the amount you earn for each sale.
- Cost per conversion: the average you spend to get one affiliate sale.

CURRENT TRENDS IN AFFILIATE MARKETING

Knowing how affiliate marketers and brands use this technique is essential. The most notable trends include:

Influencer marketing

Influencers, particularly micro-influencers, have become trendy in the affiliate marketing world. All organizations harness the ability of influencers to reach a massive audience to market their brands. Experts predict that micro-influencers will dominate the affiliate marketing sector, especially among businesses with low budgets. Moreover, buyers trust a promotion by an influencer regarded as an authority in a particular niche.

Virtual shopping

The rise of online shopping has encouraged companies to move their operations online. This provides multiple opportunities for affiliate marketing beginners to thrive. Virtual shopping is evolving towards livestream shopping, which is becoming trendy on platforms like YouTube and Twitch. Influencers provide discount codes during livestreams to drive sales to affiliate partners. This is a rising trend worth monitoring.

Social selling using video content

Video content is undoubtedly the leading trend in affiliate marketing. Platforms like TikTok, YouTube, and Instagram are mainstream ways of sharing ideas, promotions, and content. Therefore, engaging target audiences using short videos and livestreams has become an effective way of gaining views, increasing brand awareness, gaining popularity, and boosting conversion rates. Moreover, brands and influencers can engage their audience by making suggestions, asking questions, and advertising affiliate deals.

Link building and co-marketing

Link building means putting your landing page or website's link on another affiliate page. If you have more links to different pages, Google places your website higher in search results. This is not a new trend but has become popular as brands cooperate more.

Co-marketing partnerships among affiliates have also become popular. It is an excellent strategy for getting diverse audiences for products and services.

Voice search

Research has revealed that half of the affiliate traffic comes from mobile devices. Therefore, experts predict that voice-operated searches will become a mainstream way of advertising for affiliate marketing. You must create a suitable landing page with commonly asked questions and answers to venture into voice-related-search.

Crypto boom

Cryptocurrencies have become trendy in recent years. This increasing popularity means consumers are becoming more selective and demanding. Therefore, affiliate marketers should watch out for crypto affiliate programs.

CONCLUSION

Whether you consider your brand small or big, social media remains the best platform for creating brand awareness. Develop a comprehensive social media strategy to boost your brand visibility, build relationships with your prospects and establish two-way communication with your current customers.

To enjoy these benefits, you must master the fundamentals of social media marketing discussed in Chapter 2. Social media marketing has five pillars on which you should build your strategy. Therefore, ensure you have your *social strategy, planning and publishing, listening and engagement, analytics and reporting,* and *advertising* covered. You also need to understand the fundamentals of your sector's sales funnel.

With that in mind, you will need to select the social media platform you will be using. There are over 65 social media platforms, and you can't be on all of them and be effective. Wait, can you? If you have understood the chapters in this book, then you know that it is not practical. Several factors will help you select the most suitable platforms for your current strategy. The rule of thumb is to start on one platform and grow from there. In this sense, you should go for the most popular platform among your target audience.

In addition, you should also know the content type your target audience interacts with most on the platform. For example, Gen-Zers seem to love short, quirky videos. Therefore, if they are your target, you must include TikToks, Instagram Reels and YouTube Shorts in your content. The bottom line is that your target audience, content strategy and platform of choice should align.

A famous adage states that *"old is gold."* When it comes to digital marketing, email marketing is gold! Digital marketing experts agree that email marketing remains a top digital marketing approach. Therefore, incorporate this tried and tested approach to your social media marketing strategy to make it more efficient.

Additionally, it goes without saying that a modern-day business should own a website. Your website will represent your brand online. Depending on your industry, having a website will help establish your brand as an authority. It allows you to showcase different facets of your business using different content formats. It also serves as a point of convergence for all your social media content. Moreover, having a well-designed website boosts your credibility.

After all that, work on your social media marketing strategy. Using the information in Chapter 7, create a solid strategy that will help take your brand to the next level. Be open-minded when developing your strategy because it will require some chopping and changing from time to time.

In this sense, you need a formula for how you will measure your social media marketing success. Remember, your goals will help you formulate the metrics you will use to measure your performance. You can use native analytics tools found on different social media platforms, but that can be cumbersome. Therefore, take advantage of social media analytics tools to make your efforts more efficient.

Some wise men stated that the *proof of the pudding is in the eating*! In this regard, proof of your understanding will be in you creating your social media marketing strategy. Use the steps shared in Chapter 9 to create a solid social media strategy for your business. Then, use that strategy to develop a solid plan to take your company forward. Now go and take your brand to the next level!

GLOSSARY OF TERMS

AR: Real-time overlaying of virtual items in situations based on reality is made possible by AR (Artificial Reality).

AR: The real-time integration of digital information with the environment of the user is known as Augmented Reality (AR).

B2B: Business-to-business marketing, as its name suggests, refers to promoting goods and services to other corporations and enterprises.

CTA: A Call to Action, often known as a "CTA," is a request made to website visitors to perform a certain activity. Most call-to-action copy is composed as an order or imperative, such as "Sign Up Today" or "Buy Now." CTAs are shown as buttons and links.

CRM: To manage and evaluate client interactions, businesses utilize a combination of practices, strategies, and technologies known as customer relationship management (CRM).

CTRs: You can utilize click-through rates (CTR) to determine how well your free listings, advertising, and keywords perform. You calculate CTR as the number of clicks your advertisement receives divided by the number of times it is displayed.

EEPC: Electronic earnings per click are calculated by dividing your overall profits for a given period by the number of clicks you generated during that time. This offers you a rough idea of the earnings you might anticipate from every click you generate.

ESP: A service like Gmail, Outlook, or Yahoo that handles the technical aspects of sending and receiving emails is known as an email service provider.

EWOM: Conceptually, "any good or negative statement made by future, actual, or past customers about a product or firm, which is made available to a large number of people and institutions over the Internet" can be used to describe electronic word-of-mouth.

GIFs: A GIF (Graphics Interchange Format) file is a graphic image that moves on a Web page, such as a revolving emblem, a banner with a waving hand, or letters that appear to enlarge by themselves.

HTML: The most fundamental component of the Web is HTML (HyperText Markup Language). It describes the purpose and organization of web content.

KPIs: KPIs (Key Performance Indicators) are quantitative metrics used to assess the effectiveness of marketing campaigns. They are useful tools for decision-making and determining the effectiveness of your marketing investments. Therefore, the third and last step in developing a marketing strategy is to execute it.

Custom Landmarkers: "Custom Landmarkers is a feature that enables designers to create distinctive AR experiences for nearby locations they care about.

NAP: Name, address, and phone are abbreviated as NAP. The firm name, address, and phone number you use on any website where you appear are referred to as your NAP.

NBA: As a special case of next-best-action decision-making, next-best-action marketing (also known as best next action, next best activity, or recommended action) is a customer-centric marketing paradigm that weighs the various actions that can be taken for a particular customer and then decides on the best one to provide.

PPC: Pay-per-click, or PPC, is an Internet marketing strategy where advertisers are charged a fee each time one of their adverts is clicked. Essentially, it's a method of purchasing visitors to your website rather than trying to "win" those visitors naturally.

PPL: A marketer pays an affiliate, proportional to the number of converted leads they generate for the advertiser in a pay-per-lead (PPL) affiliate marketing program.

PPS: Pay-per-sale marketing, also known as cost-per-sale marketing, pays the owner or publisher of a Website by the volume of purchases brought about by an advertisement on the site. According to this arrangement, the advertiser is only responsible for paying for sales that the site generates based on a previously decided commission rate.

RED: The main goal of responsive email designs is to offer content that is tailored to the user's preferred device. You can send email templates that adapt to the size of the device being used to view them.

R3MAT: The #R3MAT Method is when the appropriate message is presented to the right person at the proper time with the appropriate expectations.

ROI: Return on investment (ROI) is a performance metric used to assess an investment's effectiveness or profitability.

SCV: The term "single customer view" (SCV) refers to a representation of customer data that is comprehensive, consistent, and aggregated.

SEO: "Search engine optimization" is known as SEO. It simply refers to making changes to your website more visible.

SMM: To develop a company's brand, boost sales, and enhance website traffic, social media marketing, often referred to as digital marketing and e-marketing, uses social media platforms where users may create social networks and share information.

SERPs: Google's response to a user's search query is displayed on search engine results pages, commonly referred to as "SERPs."

UGC: User-generated content refers to social media posts that individuals from all networks share. They are not compensated when they are talking about a good or service.

URL: Websites have individual addresses to make it easier for users to find them, just like residences and structures have street addresses. These are known as URLs on the Internet (Uniform Resource Locators).

3Vs: The three defining characteristics or dimensions of big data are the 3Vs (volume, variety, and velocity). Volume, variety, and velocity all refer to the quantity of data, the number of different sorts of data, and the rate at which the data is processed.

REFERENCES

80+ Powerful Social Media Marketing Quotes to Inspire You. (2021). Retrieved August 22, 2022, from SocialChamp website: https://www.socialchamp.io/blog/powerful-social-media-marketing-quotes/

Alfred, L. (2021). How To Create a Social Media Marketing Strategy. Retrieved August 22, 2022, from Buffer website: https://buffer.com/library/social-media-marketing-strategy/

APARNA. (2022). The Ultimate Mobile Email Open Statistics. Retrieved August 22, 2022, from easysendy website: https://easysendy.com/blog/mobile-email-open-statistics/

Baker, K. (2022). Twitter Marketing in 2021: The Ultimate Guide. Retrieved August 22, 2022, from HubSpot website: https://blog.hubspot.com/blog/tabid/6307/bid/25084/the-ultimate-cheat-sheet-for-expert-twitter-marketing.aspx

Barnhart, B. (2021). Building your social media marketing strategy for 2022. Retrieved August 22, 2022, from sproutsocial website: https://sproutsocial.com/insights/social-media-marketing-strategy/

Berg, P. (2022). Social Media SEO: Everything You Need to Know. Retrieved August 22, 2022, from Forge and Smith website: https://forgeandsmith.com/blog/social-media-seo-business/#:~:text=SEO is about optimizing your,people interested in your offering

Blain, B. (2022). Affiliate Marketing Trends for 2022. Retrieved August 22, 2022, from Printify website: https://printify.com/blog/affiliate-marketing-trends/

Brooks, A. (2022). Affiliate Marketing Made Simple: A Step-By-Step Guide. Retrieved August 22, 2022, from Venture Hub website: https://www.ventureharbour.com/affiliate-marketing-guide/

Chris, A. (2022). Website Marketing - The Complete Strategy Guide. Retrieved August 22, 2022, from RELIABLESOFT website: https://www.reliablesoft.net/website-marketing/

Coates, T.-N. (2022). Social Media. Retrieved August 9, 2022, from Britannica website: https://www.britannica.com/topic/social-media

Coleman, B. (2022). YouTube Marketing. Retrieved August 20, 2022, from HubSpot website: https://www.hubspot.com/youtube-marketing

Conley, M. (2022). Facebook Marketing. Retrieved August 18, 2022, from HubSpot website: https://www.hubspot.com/facebook-marketing

Cooper, P. (2021). How the YouTube Algorithm Works in 2022: The Complete Guide. Retrieved August 20, 2022, from Hootsuite website: https://blog.hootsuite.com/how-the-youtube-algorithm-works/

Decker, A. (2022). Instagram Marketing. Retrieved August 22, 2022, from HubSpot website: https://www.hubspot.com/instagram-marketing

Devitto, Z. (2022). Creating Your Social Media Strategy: A Step-By-Step Guide. Retrieved August 22, 2022, from ScoopIt website: https://blog.scoop.it/2022/02/15/creating-your-social-media-strategy-a-step-by-step-guide/

Dixon, S. (2022). Global social networks ranked by number of users 2022. Retrieved August 18, 2022, from Statista website: https://www.statista.com/statistics/272014/global-social-networks-ranked-by-number-of-users/

Dollarhide, M. (2021). Social Media. Retrieved August 9, 2022, from Investopedia website: https://www.investopedia.com/terms/s/social-media.asp

Dormer, L. (2021). Email marketing trends 2021- 5 trends to watch. Retrieved August 22, 2022, from Smart Insights website: https://www.smartinsights.com/email-marketing/email-marketing-trends-2021-5-trends-to-watch/

Emplifi. (2022). Social Media Analytics: The Complete Guide. Retrieved August 22, 2022, from Emplifi website: https://emplifi.io/resources/blog/social-media-analytics-the-complete-guide

Forsey, C. (2021). 10 social media trends marketers should watch in 2022 [data+expert tips]. Retrieved August 9, 2022, from HubSpot website: https://blog.hubspot.com/marketing/social-media-predictions-2017#:~:text=Social Media Trends in 2022,-TikTok will dominate&text=Augmented Reality will become consumers,advertising will become more sophisticated.

Greene, J. (2021). Social Media and SEO: How They Work Together to Boost Your Visibility. Retrieved August 22, 2022, from DataBox website: https://databox.com/social-media-and-seo

Griffin, L. (2022). Social media marketing. Retrieved August 9, 2022, from WhatIs.com website: https://www.techtarget.com/whatis/definition/social-media-marketing-SMM

Griffis, H. (2022). The Ultimate TikTok Marketing Guide. Retrieved August 20, 2022, from Buffer website: https://buffer.com/library/tiktok-marketing/

Hayes, A. (2022). Social Media Marketing (SMM). Retrieved August 9, 2022, from Investopedia website: https://www.investopedia.com/terms/s/social-media-marketing-smm.asp

Hirose, A. (2022a). 24 Pinterest Stats That Matter to Marketers in 2022. Retrieved August 20, 2022, from Hootsuite website: https://blog.hootsuite.com/pinterest-statistics-for-business/#Pinterest_usage_statistics

Hirose, A. (2022b). How To Create a Successful TikTok Marketing Strategy for 2022. Retrieved August 20, 2022, from Hootsuite website: https://blog.hootsuite.com/tiktok-marketing/

Horzewski, A. (2021). 6 tips for choosing the right social media platform for your business. Retrieved August 9, 2022, from Aventi Group website: https://aventigroup.com/blog/6-tips-for-choosing-the-right-social-media-platform-for-your-business/

Hudson, M. (2020). What is social media? Retrieved August 9, 2022, from The balance small business website: https://www.thebalancesmb.com/what-is-social-media-2890301

Instagram Marketing: The Definitive Guide (2022 update). (2022). Retrieved August 21, 2022, from Later website: https://later.com/instagram-marketing/

Kakkar, G. (2022). What are the different types of social media? Retrieved August 9, 2022, from Digital Vidya website: https://www.digitalvidya.com/blog/types-of-social-media/

Kalehoff, M. (2022). TikTok UGC and Brand Videos Outperform other Ad Formats In Driving Attention in Mobile. Retrieved August 22, 2022, from Real Eyes website: https://blog.realeyesit.com/tiktok-ugc-and-brand-videos-outperform-other-ad-formats-in-driving-attention-in-mobile

Knight, W. (2017a). How to Create a social Media Marketing Content Plan in 7 Steps. Retrieved August 9, 2022, from Social Media Examiner website: https://www.socialmediaexaminer.com/how-to-create-social-media-marketing-content-plan-in-7-steps/

Knight, W. (2017b). How to Create a Social Media Marketing Content Plan in 7 Steps. Retrieved August 22, 2022, from Social Media Examiner website: https://www.socialmediaexaminer.com/how-to-create-social-media-marketing-content-plan-in-7-steps/

Litmus. (2022). Email Marketing ROI. Retrieved August 22, 2022, from Litmus website: https://www.litmus.com/resources/email-marketing-roi/

Lozano, D. (2018). 6 Reasons Why You Need a Social Media Strategy. Retrieved August 22, 2022, from Social Media Today website: https://www.socialmediatoday.com/news/6-reasons-why-you-need-a-social-media-strategy/515622/#:~:text=Having a social media strategy,create posts which reinforce them

Lua, A. (2022). How to Use Facebook to Market Your Business. Retrieved August 19, 2022, from Buffer website: https://buffer.com/library/facebook-marketing/#facebook-algorithm

Macready, H. (2022). Snapchat for Business: The Ultimate Marketing Guide. Retrieved August 22, 2022, from Hootsuite website: https://blog.hootsuite.com/snapchat-for-business-guide/#:~:text=It connects users with brands,like Cosmopolitan magazine and MTV.

Marrs, M. (2022). 7 Ways to Use Facebook for Marketing. Retrieved August 19, 2022, from WordStream website: https://www.wordstream.com/blog/ws/2013/04/15/facebook-marketing

Martin, M. (2021). Your Complete Guide to YouTube Marketing in 2022. Retrieved August 20, 2022, from Hootsuite website: https://blog.hootsuite.com/youtube-marketing/

Martin, M. (2022). 2022 Instagram Marketing: Complete Guide +18 Strategies. Retrieved August 21, 2022, from Hootsuite website: https://blog.hootsuite.com/instagram-marketing/

McDonald, S. (2022). Email Marketing Strategy: A Data-Driven Guide. Retrieved August 22, 2022, from SuperOffice website: https://www.superoffice.com/blog/email-marketing-strategy/

McLachlan, S. (2022). 23 YouTube Stats That Matter to Marketers in 2022. Retrieved August 20, 2022, from Hootsuite website: https://blog.hootsuite.com/youtube-stats-marketers/

McLachlan, S., & Gurr, A. (2022). What is Social Commerce and Why Should Your Brand Care? Retrieved August 22, 2022, from Hootsuite website: https://blog.hootsuite.com/social-commerce/#:~:text=already hanging out.-,81%25 of shoppers,-research products on

Media, B. F. (2022). 10 Advantages of Social Media Marketing for Your Business. Retrieved August 9, 2022, from Blue Fountain Media website: https://www.bluefountainmedia.com/blog/advantages-of-social-media-marketing

Mikolajczyk, K. (2021). TikTok celebrates 1 billion users. Retrieved August 22, 2022, from Hootsuite website: https://blog.hootsuite.com/social-media-updates/tiktok/tiktok-1-billion-users/

Needle, F. (2022). 80+ Essential Social Media Marketing Statistics for 2022. Retrieved August 9, 2022, from HubSpot website: https://blog.hubspot.com/blog/tabid/6307/bid/23865/13-mind-bending-social-media-marketing-statistics.aspx

Newberry, C., & McLachlan, S. (2020). Social Media Advertising 101: How to Get the Most Out of Your Ad Budget. Retrieved August 9, 2022, from Hootsuite website: https://blog.hootsuite.com/social-media-advertising/

Olafson, K. (2021). How to Use Pinterest for Business: 8 Strategies You Need to Know. Retrieved August 20, 2022, from Hootsuite website: https://blog.hootsuite.com/how-to-use-pinterest-for-business/

Omale, G. (2021). Gartner Says Contact Center as a Service Will Hit Mainstream Adoption for Customer Service and Support Organizations in Less Than Two Years. Retrieved August 22, 2022, from gartner.com website: https://www.gartner.com/en/newsroom/press-releases/2021-09-16-gartner-says-contact-center-as-a-service-will-hit-mai

Partner, C. (2020). How to use a domain name in your digital marketing strategy. Retrieved

August 22, 2022, from Smart Insights website: https://www.smartinsights.com/digital-marketing-strategy/how-to-use-domain-name-digital-marketing-strategy/

Patel, N. (2022). Beginner's Guide to Email Marketing. Retrieved August 22, 2022, from neilpatel website: https://neilpatel.com/blog/beginners-guide-email-marketing/

Read, A. (2022). A Complete Guide to Instagram Marketing: Get the Playbook That Drives Results for Instagram's Top Profiles. Retrieved August 20, 2022, from Buffer website: https://buffer.com/library/instagram-marketing/#creating-a-content-strategy-for-instagram

Sides, G. (2022). How to set and exceed social media goals [9 examples]. Retrieved August 9, 2022, from Hootsuite website: https://blog.hootsuite.com/smart-social-media-goals/

Social Media Marketing for Businesses. (2022). Retrieved August 9, 2022, from WordStream website: https://www.wordstream.com/social-media-marketing

Storm, M. (2022). Fruitful Website Digital Marketing [4 Web Marketing Strategies]. Retrieved August 22, 2022, from WebFX website: https://www.webfx.com/blog/marketing/website-digital-marketing/

The 2022 Social Media Trends Report. (2022). Retrieved August 9, 2022, from HubSpot website: https://offers.hubspot.com/social-media-trends-report-2022?hubs_signup-url=blog.hub-spot.com%2Fmarketing%2Fsocial-media-predictions-2017&hubs_signup-cta=61%25 increase in mentions&hubs_post=blog.hubspot.com%2Fmarketing%2Fsocial-media-predictions-2017&hubs_

The 6 Types of Social Media With Examples. (2022). Retrieved August 9, 2022, from SEOPressor website: https://seopressor.com/social-media-marketing/types-of-social-media/

Thomas, T. (2022). Types of Email Marketing: 10 Emails You Should Be Sending. Retrieved August 22, 2022, from Thomas website: https://blog.thomasnet.com/types-of-email-marketing

Tien, S., & Prodanovic, K. (2022). The 9 Most Important Social Media Trends for 2022. Retrieved August 22, 2022, from Hootsuite website: https://blog.hootsuite.com/social-media-trends/

TikTok. (2022). New Studies quantify TikTok's growing impact on culture and music. Retrieved August 22, 2022, from TikTok website: https://newsroom.tiktok.com/en-us/new-studies-quantify-tiktoks-growing-impact-on-culture-and-music

Tomas, D. (2022). What are Social Media Ads? Examples and Types of Social Media Advertising. Retrieved August 9, 2022, from Cyberclick website: https://www.cyberclick.net/numerical blogen/what-exactly-are-social-ads-types-and-examples-of-advertising-on-social-media

Vaughan, P. (2022). Why List Segmentation Matters in Email Marketing. Retrieved August 22, 2022, from HubSpot website: https://blog.hubspot.com/blog/tabid/6307/bid/32848/Why-List-Segmentation-Matters-in-Email-Marketing.aspx?__hstc=163636576.6877ca8675c062ef b658e97ec6800b1f.1642147270159.1645004623034.1645009927517.58&__hssc=163636576.1. 1645009927517&__hsfp=263415764

Wagner, J. (2021). Social Media Organic Reach 2021: Who actually sees your content? Retrieved August 18, 2022, from Ignite Social Media website: https://www.ignitesocialmedia.com/social-media-strategy/social-media-organic-reach-2021-who-actually-sees-your-content/

What is social media marketing? (2022). Retrieved August 9, 2022, from Buffer website: https://buffer.com/social-media-marketing

Whitney, M. (2022). 6 strategies to Improve Your Social Media Marketing Plan. Retrieved August 22, 2022, from WordStream website: https://www.wordstream.com/blog/ws/2015/01/19/social-media-marketing-plan

Wong, J. (2021). How to Optimize Your Content For SEO And Social Media Marketing. Retrieved August 22, 2022, from Forbes website: https://www.forbes.com/sites/forbescommunication scouncil/2021/08/02/how-to-optimize-your-content-for-seo-and-social-media-marketing/? sh=30e65d2d55c2

Printed in Great Britain
by Amazon

16311454R00102